The History Of
Valley Park
Through The 20th Century

Ken Curtis

© 2010 Meramec Valley Historical Society

ISBN 10: 1-893937-44-5
ISBN 13: 978-1-893937-44-4

All Rights Reserved Under
International and Pan-American Copyright Conventions.
No part of this book may be used or reproduced in any manner
whatsoever without written permission except in the case of brief
quotations embodied in critical articles or reviews.

Printed in the United States by
Independent Publishing Corporation
St. Louis, Missouri 63021

Table of Contents

It Might Have Been Spanish Or French 1

Early Settlement 4

The City Becomes a City 15

Focus On Early People And Updates 25

Medicines, Medicine Men And A Medicine Woman 34

Education 41

Early 1900's 51

The Dirty Thirties 60

The Forties 89

Long Term Perspectives 113

A Success Story 133

Student Historians 138

More City Business 175

Personal Note 182

Post Script 186

Through The 20th Century

In 1953 in the Headquarters of Divarty, Camp Roberts, California, it was getting closer to sundown. I was charge of quarters for the evening/night beginning my watch. The windows were open and wind rustled through branches and leaves outside the headquarters building. I penned the following thoughts as a tide of memories spilled over and around me about my home town – Valley Park.

An Autumn Itinerary

As autumn's leaves stretch out their fingers
And sketched their awkward patterns on the ground
My mind drifts swiftly, pauses, and then lingers-
As through the trembling branches comes a sound.
I listen! And hear a school bell ringing,
And see a mother dandling a child
Then cuddle him the meanwhile softly singing
A lullaby and then she stops and smiles.
I wander past the stores hard by the train tracks,
By a creek bed where a cool stream tumbles down
And far from parent spring meets rolling river
Which lines the southern limits of the town.
From the auto span I gaze downstream
Where rails catch rays of sun
And girders rest on piers o'er which
The railroad cargoes run
The horizon line grows dimmer, then dark,

The History Of Valley Park

As earth's mother star slips down.
My daydream dissipates and I'm awake now –
Awake and far away from my home town
                    …Ken Curtis

Through The 20th Century

ACKNOWLEDGEMENTS

Acknowledgements to make this effort possible are due to those whose names appear in the various accounts. In other words this is a history which comes in large part from the people who lived it, and for those who gave secondary source accounts from earlier generations. A special recognition is appropriate for Eileen Sherrill, history teacher, and her students in Valley Park High along with Marlene Hedrick and the members of the Meramec Valley Historical Society.

The author has had the opportunity of personal acquaintance with almost all of those who furnished information about themselves, but must give credit to students of Valley Park Schools for their interest as participants in interviews with many Valley Park residents. Their teachers – Lisa Gross, Helen Jones Gansler, Doris Jones Waplehorst, Dorothy Bright Kassler, and Sue Robinson also deserve recognition.

Special thanks is given to Fairy May (Steele) Hollerich for her account of early telephone service and for information

The History Of Valley Park

on a number of her contemporaries, including the way in which the author might contact them for information.

This effort confines itself to life and times up to around the end of the Twentieth Century. It was necessary to establish a cut off to avoid a continuous account that would never be finalized in any way and published. There is some effort to establish a chronological account but this is interrupted in the case of individual memories which traverse the lifetimes of some of the primary and secondary sources.

Thanks to Marguerite Wilburn for assistance in pouring over Board of Aldermen minutes and to Don Smith who helped locate some of these for use.

A big thank you to Margot Dersham for uncovering repetitions, other glitches and erroneous entries in the initial manuscript.

Through The 20th Century

IT MIGHT HAVE BEEN SPANISH OR FRENCH

The tract of land is located upstream from the Mississippi on the banks of the Meramec. Highway 141 crosses the Meramec, which flows eastward at that crossing. The land is part of the Louisiana Territory, named after the French monarch. Nations fought over control of the land as nations often do.

Near the end of the French and Indian War, so named because the French and Indian Tribes friendly to the French fought the English, it became apparent that England would prevail.

By the terms of the Treaty of Paris, 1763, France was ousted from control but in hopes of preventing English control of the continent, France ceded the territory to Spain prior to the treaty. Spain held primary control until 1800 when Napoleon, in control of many European affairs, twisted the arm of the Spanish Catholic Majesty of Spain and had the land ceded to France under the Treaty of St. Ildefonso. In 1783, the American Colonies won independence from Britain and became the United States of America. The Mississippi was the primary western boundary of the new

The History Of Valley Park

United States, but where the Mississippi emptied into the Gulf of Mexico, both sides of the Mississippi were controlled by France. This was a problem for the westerners who wanted to ship goods on the high seas and had to go through New Orleans.

They needed a port of deposit to store goods prior to loading on the ocean going vessels with their unpredictable arrivals. Thomas Jefferson dispatched negotiators to France to try to arrange for the purchase of such a port. Imagine their surprise when Napoleon offered to sell the entire Louisiana Territory. Napoleon had seen Santo Domingo in the Caribbean as a staging area for his mission to rebuild French influence in North America. His efforts in Santo Domingo were resisted by yellow fever among his troops and the leadership of Touissant l'Overture, who organized the native population against the French. And so it was that a little black man in Santo Domingo had much to do with the United States acquiring the land west of the Mississippi in 1803, including the area where Highway 141 crosses the Meramec River.

The area had been inhabited by the Osage Indians, who left many of their artifacts in the area. The Indians often carried out hunting and foraging excursions upstream on the Meramec to where an overland trek to the Missouri River was not too distant, and then returned downstream

Through The 20th Century

on the Missouri and Mississippi. Then they went upstream on the Meramec to where 141 crosses the river and where industrialists would capitalize on a major asset of the area.

The History Of Valley Park

EARLY SETTLEMENT

White settlers began moving into the area in limited numbers in the early 1800's before Missouri became a state in 1821. Later in the century, many would find the area an attractive playground. A "Dupree" map in 1838 shows St. Louis County divided into five townships – Meramec to the west, Bonhomme in the primarily central sector, St. Ferdinand farthest north, St. Louis (south of St. Ferdinand) and Carondolet immediately south of St. Louis Township. The latter three townships made up the eastern sector of St. Louis County and bordered the Mississippi.

The City of St. Louis was established in 1875 as a charter city with the status of a county. This divorced St. Louis City from St. Louis County.

John Dougherty started a ferry service across the Meramec and past the Dougherty farm, purchased by the Doughertys in 1826, along with other tracts toward the ferry crossing. This route became Dougherty Ferry Road and was later known as Forest Avenue inside the City of Valley Park. Shortly thereafter, a road which joined Dougherty Ferry a short distance from the crossing became the county road to Manchester. This later became Meramec Station Road, derived from the earlier name of Valley Park which was known as Meramec Station. Captain Taylor, owner of a steamboat company, purchased the ferry operation and some adjacent land and continued to operate the ferry.

John Dougherty died in 1835 after a number of treatments for a tumor in his mouth. The frequent lancings of the tumor did not achieve a cure. Several doctors attended him at different times – Dr. R. B. Harris, Dr. A. A. Harman, Dr. M. Young, and Dr. Peter Kinkeade. Dougherty had taken a loan from Ann Biddle, a sister-in-law of Nicolas Biddle, the President of the Bank of the United States. (President Jackson called the bank "Biddle's Monster" and vowed he would kill the monster). Ann was the the widow of Major Thomas Biddle (brother of Nicolas) who had purchased 170 acres of land in Valley Park although it is unclear whether he ever lived there. Thomas was killed in a duel with Senator Spencer Pettis, following a challenge to the Senator's seat by Biddle in a down and dirty, mud-slinging campaign which Pettis won handily. The duel took place on "Bloody Island" in the Mississippi on August 27, 1831, and having agreed that the distance between them would be five feet on command to fire, both fell mortally wounded. Ann Biddle sued the estate of John Dougherty for the $600 owed her and his property was sold in a public sale ordered by the Court of the City of St. Louis. (We must remember that St. Louis was the county seat of St. Louis County until St. Louis City detached itself from the County in 1875).

In the days prior to the Civil War, stories handed down by old timers, tell us that a resident to the south and east of what is now Valley Park, used the community as a place to visit for recreational purposes and to impress an object of his affection, Julia Dent. That was Ulysses S. Grant, who would later become President of the United States. By the mid-1870's roughly half a century after Missouri became a state, two trains per day were running to and from the area, then known as Meramec Station, and the pleasure seekers from the more populated areas to the east, found what they sought in the clear, free flowing Meramec and lakes with swimming and boating the more popular pursuits. The train schedules were published in the *St. Louis Republic*, a newpaper of the period.

Long time residents tell of stories relayed by Kirkwood residents about how they would board the train in Kirkwood, making sure to be in the last car on the train. Then, as the train slowed, they would jump from the train and avoid the conductor who collected tickets and/or fares. The conductor seldom reached the last car before the train stopped. The freeloaders used the same tactics on their return home after taking part in the usual recreational activities.

Through The 20th Century

Prior to the Civil War, a wagon bridge across the Meramec eliminated the need for the ferry service. The bridge joined areas south of the Meramec like Fenton and Hillsboro with Valley Park and Manchester.

Gerhardt H. Timmerman had made a modest fortune in his foundry business in St. Louis furnishing Civil War materials. He started the first mill at the site on 141 close by the railroad tracks in 1874 and the mill was restored each time after a number of fires. In 1895, The Valley Park Elevator adjacent the mill site, began turning out casks, barrels, and other containers. At one time the mill produced a "White Rose" brand of graham flour, corn meal and feed. Increasing numbers of people became permanent residents. The community soon boasted a U. S. Post Office which was sometimes referred to as Nasby Post Office. In 1876 Postmaster G. B. Summer had named the post office Meramec. Two years later, the next Postmaster, Henry B. Milks, named it Nasby. It's a guess that Milks wanted to honor columnist/humorist, Petroleum V. Nasby, the pen name for David R. Locke. He wrote material critical and satirical about the southern viewpoint and Milks, sympathizing with the North in the Civil War, wanted to strike a blow against pro-southern sentiment which prevailed in Valley Park where a number of slaveholders had lived. George Berry, who became Postmaster in 1888, gave the Post Office its

The History Of Valley Park

current name, Valley Park, to conform with the name for which the town had come to be known.

At the St. Louis World's Fair, surrey topped boats gave fairgoers a ride around the Grand Basin and after the Fair, some of those surrey top boats were seen giving visitors in Valley Park a ride on the Meramec River. Lumber salvaged from pavilions on the fairgrounds came to Valley Park in some quantities and were used to build houses along with other uses. The World's Fair had an afterglow in Valley Park as it did in a number of communities.

Preceding and beyond the decade of the 1900's it was not uncommon to see families camped in tents on the banks of the Meramec. A young man who had a boat would find that he could attract young ladies to outings and it was not unknown for a young man or two to engage in a bit of deceit in claiming to own a boat and then being jilted when a lady of interest to him discovered the untruth.

By the end of the 19th Century, Valley Park had gained area-wide recognition as a playground but a big change was coming. At the turn of the Century, newcomers began quietly buying up property and the townsfolk knew something was up. A good guess might have been that a big resort development was underway since the area had already become popular as a playground. But it was not

Through The 20th Century

the recreational features which attracted the newcomers. It was that sand in the Meramec and the sub-terrain of the Meramec's banks. Eastern business interests (some said associates of Andrew Carnegie) had decided to utilize that fine Meramec sand in a gigantic glass making operation. To do so, at lowest cost, a readily available supply of labor was necessary. As businesses were known to do, they would seek a major influence in the community. Valley Park became one of the later "company towns." The Valley Park Land Company laid out a grid work of lots along Marshall Road. Here was where the workers in the glass making operation would be housed. Farther north, along Benton Street and Leonard, the residences of managers would be located. It all seemed like a good idea at the time. So, while St. Louis was focusing on the World Fair, interests in Valley Park were getting ready for a glass making operation that would dwarf any other.

All the new buildings would be collectively referred to as "newtown," a term which for many years, newer residents and new generations did not understand unless they were acquainted with the City's history

The modest buildings along Marshall were soon filled with occupants whose calling was to convert Meramec sand into glass for use throughout the nation. The glass making operation often demanded a Herculean effort. Those tending

The History Of Valley Park

the furnaces and the molten glass through the annealing process to the finished product went about their work as though possessed by demons throughout the two twelve hour shifts. Even so, the jobs were prized by those who had them and recent immigrants from Europe lived in tents along the Meramec, hoping to find work in the factory. Child labor was openly exploited and a long time resident, Warren Henlon, recalled how proud he was at the age of twelve to work his twelve hour shift in the factory polishing room and emerge with his skin and clothing rouge colored, hoping people would notice him.

In addition to the glass factory construction and the housing for workers and managers, the Valley Park Land Company built the Valley Park Hotel just to the northeast of Didian Avenue and close to the later elevated Missouri Pacific Railroad. An April 10, 1909, Vol. 23, Special Edition of the *Valley Park Sun* carried a glowing account of that hotel:

The Valley Park Hotel, known as the "Big Hotel on the Hill," is one of the greatest attractions of "the best in the west." The magnificent modern building was erected by the Valley Park Land Company at a cost of $75,000 and opened to the public in 1904. It is surrounded by a most beautiful and tastefully arranged park, sloping gently southward, where the "cooling breezes" of the Meramec valley (in the

Through The 20th Century

spring and summer) are wafted over carpets of blue grass and through rare, variegated shrubbery and perfume-laden flowers.

It contains over forty rooms, besides two parlors, halls, a ball room and a dining room. The building is steam-heated, has electric lights and other modern arrangements and conveniences.

The broad veranda extending along the entire front and east and west wings of the building is crowded in summer by the numerous pleasure seeking visitors, who come to enjoy the attractions and peacefulness of progressive Valley Park.

The spring and summer months constitute the hotel's busy season. Valley Park is situated at the end of the best automobile run out of St. Louis, and this makes the "Big Hotel on the Hill" a popular resort for automobile parties.

The magnificent hotel is a never-ceasing advertisement for the town, and a monument to the munificence and public spirit of its builders and owners.

The Meramec River, which had watched quietly while the community was growing, reacted to heavy August rainfall in 1915 and escaped its channel to invade the surrounding

The History Of Valley Park

adjacent plain. The waters rushed into and through the glass factory, destroying much of the operation. Following that, the *St. Louis Republic* newspaper quoted plant superintendent Albright saying the workers, "...will likely be without work for two weeks, and possibly a month." Those workers were never paid for their last week of work.

One of those who held an interest in glassmaking, Robert Dubuquenany, along with some of his associates, reopened the factory and resumed glassmaking. In 1916, though, a fire swept through the factory destroying three-fourths of the equipment and the plant was closed forever. The demand for glass had diminished. Capilalists who might otherwise have revived the operation put their money into war materials, the demand for which was growing and promising greater profits with WWI war clouds gathering. Bob Vance furnished the information about the little known re-opening of the glass factory and its being shuttered permanently. In the final chapter of the one time largest plate glass factory in the world, the property was sold on the steps of the St. Louis County Courthouse in Clayton on June 25,1925. The brick crucibles and tunnels, covered with sediment from a number of Meramec overflows, for many years furnished an attractive nuisance and source for injury for the young. Many youngsters found their way into the underground caverns and treated them as a playground.

Through The 20th Century

William Rue was among those youngsters in the 1930's. He noted that quite a number of kids were hurt playing in the area but it did not keep them away. "I have spent many an hour playing and exploring the grounds when I was twelve years old," he said.

In the 1970's the land occupied by the old glass factory was acquired by the Harrawood family, which had a construction business and a more recent interest in owning and operating an athletic complex on the site. The Harrawood Brothers became the owners of a professional women's softball team, the St. Louis Hummers. There were good crowds at the Hummer games but financial difficulties in some of the league teams in other cities caused the league to fold. Ron Jacober, who became a well known sports commentator in radio, got some of his earliest experiences as a field announcer for the Hummer games. Linda Wells was a catcher for the Hummers and she was the daughter of Blanche (Hess) Wells, a resident as a youth of Valley Park who later moved to Pacific. Linda was the women's athletic director at the University of Minnesota.

At the end of the Twentieth Century, the land was still a site of athletic activity, showing no sign that base paths were once tread by men carrying a huge plate of glass, listening for a ping, signaling that a break/shattering was

The History Of Valley Park

about to occur, and at that signal, dropping the plate to run a safe distance away.

Through The 20th Century

THE CITY BECOMES A CITY

May 5, 1917, a group of townspeople met in one of two schools, the South School, at the top of Meramec Station where Fern Ridge intersects it.

This was not a Board of Education meeting, but a meeting of the Mayor and Board of Aldermen who had moved to have the City incorporated. W. T. Vance was Mayor. W. H. James, J. A. Meyers, William Wood, S. S. Inman, William Boly, H. G. Arnold, Marten Schmann, and S. H. Dietrich were Aldermen. Charles Mockaby was City Clerk. Frank P. Knabb was City Clerk. J. O. Sturdy was Marshal. None of these were elected but in the Articles of Incorporation were listed except for the three appointees, as officials of the City until such time as an election would be held. This was one of the longest, and may have been the longest Board of Aldermen meeting. The minutes of that meeting, written in longhand as would be the case for some time, took nine pages of legal sized paper. The appointments of Treasurer, City Clerk and Marshal took place.

On the heels of the great flood, there was no longer financing of any public services by the Valley Park Land

Company and there needed to be a means to provide those services. This was the probable reason for the City's incorporation. For the City's first month of operation, the expenses were $2 for rent and $.31 for the Collector or a total of $2.31. An appreciation was expressed to W. T. Vance for providing chairs to the "overworked and underpaid members of the Board of Aldermen."

The next meeting was scheduled for May 25, 1917, at 8:00 p.m. J. Meyers, Chair of Finance Ways and Means Committee, introduced proposed ordinance No. 1, a measure to levy a tax of 25 cents on the $100 assessed valuation. That measure was given its necessary readings and passed unanimously.

On January 4, 1918, the Mayor was authorized to issue notes against the treasury of the City in amounts of $25 and $100 to pay for the installation of a gas pumping facility and costs associated with it. There were grumbles about the exorbitant price which was bid by the Automatic Gas Power Company.

The bills making the pumping facility operational were:

Installing transformers	$203.16
Electric Service advance	$92.04
Delivery of pump	$3.00
Installing pump	$20.50
Total	$319.70

Through The 20th Century

On April 8, 1918, the City held its first election. W.T. Vance received 30 votes for Mayor, Robert A. Sargent received 36 and J. Meyer received one. John Sturdy was elected Collector and James O'Brien was elected as Marshal. Elected to the Board of Aldermen were: W. James and W.T. Vance-Ward one, S. S. Inman and J. A. Meyer-Ward two, Charles Scholl and William Lloyd-Ward three and William E. Schumann and H. G. Arnold-Ward four. The reader might note that two of the elected Aldermen had also been candidates for Mayor.

Outside of City government, in 1913, Valley Park wage earners had to pay a tax based on an income formula thanks to the 16th Amendment ratified after having been proposed in 1909. In 1917 the Valley Park Postmaster, James S. Herrington, noted that he had unclaimed mail for the week ending September 22. The mail belonged to Miss Mae Kaufman, Mr. R. F. Allen, Mrs Mary Knickerbocker, Mr. and Mrs. F. S. Williams, Mr. S. K. Whitt, and Mr. Max Steel. This information was published in the Valley Park Sun along with an obituary noting the death of Booker Richardson who died "after a lingering illness. The cause of his death was senility."

The prohibitionists found momentum for their cause with the coming of WW I. The Anti-Saloon League, formed in 1893, was joined in its efforts by the Women's Christian

Temperance Union. We have already noted the presence of the WCTU in Valley Park by reference to organizations whose names were printed in the Valley Park Sun.

A story was circulated about a law passed in Missouri requiring each teacher in Missouri schools to devote at least one lesson each year to the evils of alcohol. The law was studiously ignored but one teacher decided to obey it and gathered her third grade students around a little table in the front of the room. There was a worm in the center of a saucer and the teacher poured a capful of whiskey over the worm which went through a series of agonizing movements and then lay quite still. The teacher picked up the worm twice and then dropped it. It was obviously dead. "Now", she said, "what do we learn from this demonstration?" Timmy was flapping his hand so the teacher called on him. Timmy said, "It proves that if you drink plenty of liquor, you'll never get worms."

The name, "Roaring Twenties" as the designation for the 1920's decade was not universal. It was also known as the "Jazz Age" and in Valley Park it was featured by some businesses similar to the speak easies, requiring some special recognition for admission. In Valley Park, the arrangement was somewhat different since most businesses knew most of their patrons, residents and otherwise. One of the more prominent establishments was Hotell Hodnett, discussed in more detail later.

Returning to City Hall, by the mid 1918's, minutes of the Board of Aldermen began referring to the regular meeting place of the Board at 25 Marshall Road, probably rented until October 3, 1921. On that date, John Goree moved and Harry Arnold seconded a motion to buy a City Hall with an addition to house a fire station at a cost of $5000. That motion carried unanimously. The City Hall was located on the south of Marshall Avenue in the middle of the block east of 141.

Aldermen and other officials had interesting assignments in the twenties. On June 27, 1922, the City was planning a picnic for July 22. The Mayor handed out the assignments. John Goree and Fred Coleman were to get donations to obtain the services of an orchestra. Art Heinemann was to get donations of cakes and chickens. Harry Arnold was to get fish. John Sturdy was to supervise activities on the dance floor and Fred Coleman was to get hams.

For a time, the picnic was an annual event. On June 12, 1923, the Board met and determined that a fiddling contest should be held at the annual picnic and a $20 prize awarded the best fiddler.

The History Of Valley Park

At a subsequent meeting a resolution was passed to be sent to the Missouri Highway Department requesting that a state highway be constructed through Moselle, Catawissa, Pacific, Allenton, Eureka, Valley Park, Sugar Creek, Kirkwood, Glendale, Webster Groves, and Maplewood. Part of the resolution stated that this would be of benefit to citizens of all these communities since the Meramec Valley is the "playground for St. Louis County." It was to be sent to the press and the Highway Commission. That resolution was signed by Mayor Robert P. Sargent.

Outside City Hall, if the Meramec could talk, it could tell a story of an inglorious moment in Valley Park involving the bridge, built following the Civil War. A man of color was found hanging off the bridge in the early part of the Twentieth Century and a number of people thought they knew who took part in the lynching but no one ever came forward and Deputy Sheriff Sturdy made no arrest. This unfortunate and inhumane scenario was repeated in many communities. The Meramec continued its flow and its sometime invasion of the adjacent plain but restoration was much simpler (though unpleasant) than was the case when waters wreaked havoc on a huge economic enterprise.

August 29, 1922, a resolution was passed by the City setting annual salaries for Mayor at $100 per year, $50 for

Aldermen, $150 for City Clerk, $600 for Marshal, $150 for Treasurer, and $180 for City Attorney.

The July 14, 1924, minutes of the Board noted the need to purchase road building equipment. A committee recommended and the Board authorized the purchase of a Fordson grader and "scarofier". The equipment was to be purchased from a firm called the Johnson Auto Company and the Mayor was authorized to execute a note of $1200 to be paid off when sufficient revenues were received. The note bore a 6% interest. On August 24, the Board authorized private party use of that equipment by paying the City $25 per day, with the City furnishing the operator(s) and the gas and oil.

Discussion "went to the dogs" at the December 26, 1924, meeting of the Board. It was mandated that the Marshal make a survey of "…dogs running at large…" without a dog tag and the Marshal was authorized "…to shoot any dog found not to be wearing a tag". The Marshal was to receive five cents for each dog disposed of under this directive.

Valley Park had an enviable position regarding railroading. There were two railroads with reciprocal switching – The Frisco and Missouri Pacific. Of course there were sometimes problems with any asset. Trains sometimes blocked intersections for prolonged periods of time and an

The History Of Valley Park

ordinance passed October 22, 1926, prohibited a train from blocking a street crossing within the City limits for longer than five minutes. A requirement in the ordinance provided that there must be "…a person on the car most distant from the engine to warn about braking and give appropriate signals." A fine of not less than five dollars nor more than fifty dollars would be imposed for any violation.

Mayor William Young offered his resignation on December 5, 1930. "Permit me," he said, "to tender my sincere thanks and appreciation to the Board of Aldermen and the citizens for the wonderful support and cooperation shown during my term of office." W. T. Vance became acting Mayor. On March 6, 1931, the office of Police Judge changed from an elective to an appointive position. The Mayor was to appoint with the approval of the Board of Aldermen.

The following August 7, that ordinance authorizing the Marshal to shoot dogs not properly tagged was revoked and a substitute ordinance, much less severe, imposed fines for violations which could be verified. Robert Sargent resigned as Police Judge in 1931 and the Mayor appointed Victor Girard to Sargent's unexpired term. In that same year, an ordinance was passed prohibiting any child under age sixteen from "…traversing the City streets without a parent or guardian or other suitable chaperone…" accompanying.

Warren Henlon, who worked as a youngster in the glass factory, served for a time as Alderman in the thirties representing the Second Ward. Financial obligations were a problem in the "dirty thirties" and on August 4, 1933, the Board authorized the Mayor to borrow up to $1500 because the "…City of Valley Park is in need of up to $1500 to pay necessary obligations." The Mayor was to obtain a note from the Meramec Valley Bank obligating the City to repay at 6% interest in three months. This anticipated revenue which would be forthcoming near the end of the year. In the following November it was moved that "…the City pay the following bills," shown on a statement, "as soon as sufficient money is on hand."

The Board seemed to have difficulty deciding which arrangement should be used for filling the office of Police Judge and on December 1, 1933, the Board approved a measure discontinuing the practice of the office being an appointment and made it an elective office.

Away from the official business, Connie Jones was writing a brief history of Valley Park in which she makes mention of her father, Glenn Jones. He was an attorney with an address on Benton Street. The phone directory listed the number 102 J for Glenn Jones. Connie noted that the City had an assessed valuation of one million dollars. Connie's history, printed in the Valley High School newspaper, the

The History Of Valley Park

Valley Breeze, tells of a contest sponsored by the local Chamber of Commerce to solicit slogans for the City and the winning slogan was "The City of Opportunity."

In the 1930's a dam was proposed upstream to make the Meramec more friendly but the project was delayed and eventually stymied by the failure of support (or outright opposition) of Congressman Clarence Cannon. That failure and the coming of WWII shelved the project because federal monies would not be forthcoming. During the 1970's it appeared that a proposed dam upstream to form a Meramec Park Lake would remove most of Valley Park from the one hundred year flood plain. Designs were completed and land purchased but environmentalists organized opposition and brought about a referendum in the Meramec Valley. The Sierra Club worked with Senator John Danforth in registering opposition to the project. It failed to receive voter support and died. In 1982 another disastrous flood took place and increased interest in finding a way to control the sometimes unfriendly Meramec. Approaching the Twenty First Century, Valley Park had underway the construction of a levy to shield main parts of the City from flooding. It is a stroke of irony that the old glass factory was not included in the area to be protected. The complex was purchased by the City for the levy with hopes of finding an entity to maintain an adjacent facility for athletic purposes.

Through The 20th Century

FOCUS ON EARLY PEOPLE AND UPDATES

A number of people provided a secondary source on early residents and a greater number provided a primary source, usually through relating personal experience. Valley Park's population dropped from 4,500 in 1915 to just 360 in a year after the great flood.

Amongst the classified ads in the Valley Park Sun, September 22, 1917, was an ad which read: "LOST – Ten Dollar Bill, last Sunday between Bank Bldg. And D'Arostinas Store. Finder please return to The Sun office and receive liberal reward."

In the 1920 Census, Valley Park could boast of prominent individuals in St. Louis County far out of proportion to its then population of 899. Robert Lang moved to Valley Park in 1917, the year the City was incorporated, and set up business in the Frisco Hotel, the building still standing at the end of the Twentieth Century west of the old Frisco Railroad and north of Marshall Avenue. He brought experience in hotel business from Cincinnati, acquired after leaving his New Orleans birthplace. After five years he moved to St. Louis in 1888 where he pursued the same interest and gained a

The History Of Valley Park

reputation as an accomplished chef. He operated a St. Louis restaurant from 1912 to 1917 and then moved to Valley Park. Mr. Lang's wife, whom he married in 1895, was the former Felicity Gobro, a native of St. Genevieve, Missouri. She had the responsibility of handling the office work. Their son, Frederick R., was attending Cornell University in Ithaca, N. Y. in 1920.

Born March 4, 1854, in Upland, Delaware County, Pennsylvania, William J. Vance organized the Valley Park Trust Company and was its president until 1917 when he disposed of his stock holdings. In 1903 he was made manager and treasurer of the St. Louis Plate Glass Company and held the position until 1914 when he resigned. In 1916 he resumed the position until 1917 when the company was sold to the Missouri Plate Glass Company.

The latter company failed that year with Mr. Vance appointed as receiver and serving as such until 1918. He had wed the former Mary Meyer of Pennsylvania in 1880. In January, 1918, he was a participant in the organization of the Meramec Valley Bank and served as cashier and Vice-President with a son Harry as assistant cashier. Harry would later become bank president and W. J. Vance (he preferred initials to William J.) served subsequently as the third Mayor of Valley Park. Officers of Meramec Bank at the close of business on December 7, 1920, were Senator

Through The 20th Century

Richard F. Ralph-President, W. J. Vance-Vice President and Cashier, Harry E. Vance-Assistant Cashier, Robert P. Sargent, Milton Wolf and Charles C. Scholl-Directors. At the close of business on the date indicated, the assets were listed as $106,083.30, an amount which seems paltry at this writing but was quite impressive for a bank of that time which had only been in business for two years.

In 1917, a boat building operation on the Meramec was begun by George B. Barbour who had earlier started a similar business in St. Louis in 1909 after a few years in retirement. He had worked in the hardware business with his father, Ormand, in Carbondale, Illinois, and bought the business in 1895. He had come to St. Louis after a brief stay in East St. Louis. His boat business specialized in construction of metal life boats and for some time had government contracts, helped no doubt by our nation's entry into WWI in 1917 when he started the Valley Park business. He branched out to build many types of boats which were sold all over the world. His boat yard and launch were located in close proximity to where the railroad bridge crosses the Meramec. Mr. Barbour's wife was the former Grace E. Munger, whom he married in 1894. They had a son and daughter, Charles M. and Frances M.

In the Meramec Valley Bank on Marshall, there is a painting by an artist named McHugh of the dock where the

The History Of Valley Park

Barbour operation was located, showing among other parts of the painting, a sailor in his white uniform.

At the age of 17, Max Waplehorst arrived in the U. S. from Westphalia, Germany. He had a stay in St. Charles, where he resided at the outbreak of the Civil Was and was enrolled in the Twenty Seventh Missouri Militia. In the later years of the war he located in St. Louis and in 1865 married Johanna Koehring, a union which produced ten children. In 1866 he came to Valley Park and was in charge of a saw mill. Two years later, he purchased farmland and a steam thresher which was something of an innovation in the area. He had the honor of being the only St. Louis County resident to receive a silver medal for wheat at the St. Louis World Fair. The bridesmaid and groomsman from the 1865 marriage, Catherine and John Timmerman, were present in 1915 when the Wapelhorsts celebrated their Golden Wedding Anniversary.

To the east and slightly north of Valley Park where the land rises to higher ground bordering Kirkwood, Meramec Highlands was an amusement park which attracted patrons from the surrounding area as well as Valley Park. Readily accessible by street car lines, this amusement park featured a large dance hall and many other attractions. The entrepeneur behind this operation was Arthur L. Autenrieth, who began as owner-manager in 1908. He had already operated a number of restaurants and refreshment stands throughout the County. That dance pavillion was described as one known to thousands of dancers and according to the *Watchman Advocate* publication of 1920 had "...the roomiest and best-surfaced dancing floor in the State."

A short journey to Valley Park was taken by Fred Coleman, a butcher and stockman who was born in High Ridge, Missouri, July 29, 1867. He went to work for his father, Nicolas Coleman, in agriculture although Nicolas was a stone mason by trade. At age 18, Fred went to Fenton as a butcher and began purchasing cattle. A butcher shop business with brother Andrew was opened in 1893 under the name, Coleman Brothers. Andrew bought out Fred's interest and Fred moved to Herman, Missouri, where he had a similar business. His brother Andrew was killed accidentally in 1904 and Fred Coleman bought out Andrew's widow and moved to Valley Park. He purchased a building and dealt in cattle, always doing his own butchering. An ad of his appeared in the September 29, 1917 Valley Park Sun. The ad read: "Fred Colman (his surname was misspelled), dealer in Beef Cattle, Hogs and Poultry Best Fresh and Cured Meats, Lard, Sausage, Etc. Vegetables and Fruits in Season Highest Cash Prices Paid for Live Stock and Country Produce". His deliveries of meat products extended over a radius of four miles.

The History Of Valley Park

He had married Emma Haeffner September 17, 1893, and they were parents of Irene E., Homer H., and Eustazia H.

The Eggers Milling Company operated mills in Valley Park, Herman, and Grafton, South Dakota, and the officers of the company were H. B. Eggers-president, H.B. Eggers,Jr.-vice president, F. W. Eggers-treasurer, and C. F. Eggers-secretary. Charles F. Eggers, secretary, managed the Valley Park operation in 1920 after it purchased the Valley Park Milling Company. Popularly known as "The Mill" for many years, the building housing the operation was still standing at this writing where it stood since its beginning – close to the railroad viaduct of the old Missouri Pacific Railroad. It was altered by the elimination of a corner when the Missouri Department of Transportation built a new highway into town and made a six lane traffic artery. Early changes in the facility eliminated a structure immediately south, leaving the existing structure with the extended smaller upper story. A porch like extension to the south was added to replace the entry which formerly was located on the west, trimmed by the new highway.

As of 1975, there were 33 stockholders in the V. P. Elevator with the main holder being Bill Osgood. In that year, the operation was purchased by Richard Grellner, who, with his sons, continued the business. Once primarily a milling operation it has become mostly a hardware store but does occasional milling. It is the only working mill in St. Louis County. Grellner's wife is the former Gloria Jean Shepherd. Richard Grellner served for a number of years as Municipal Judge in Valley Park.

E. L. Magruder, born in Brunswick, Missouri, March 23, 1868, went to Chicago at age 18 to an apprentice study as decorator. After working there 12 years he spent eight years in and finally ran a paint and wallpaper business in Valley Park He dreamed of a great amusement park and in 1912 disposed of his paint and wallpaper business and purchased a fifty acre tract east of Dougherty Ferry Road (Forest Avenue) between the old Missouri Pacific and old Frisco railroad tracks. From a small clubhouse the first year, he added improvements until the two spring fed lakes on the property were complimented with a dance pavilion which extended out over the larger lake and the twenty foot wide promenade around it. The open air swimming pool was billed as the largest in the State, 172 feet by 160 feet, having a gradually sloping bottom from shallow part to deep. It was a complete resort with picnic benches and the lakes were stocked with fish. Many swore the spring fed lake waters were good for curing various ailments ("upholding of the physically weak and rundown."), good for drinking and good for bathing. A drilling in 1919 was responsible for the flow of a hundred gallons of water per minute. Mr. Magruder

The History Of Valley Park

was married to Louise Hinze of Madison, Iowa, August 3, 1894, and she and their two sons assisted in managing the operation.

Throughout the earlier Twentieth Century, Arnold's Landing was another fvorite attraction to pleasure seekers in Valley Park and the vicinity. Harry Arnold was born in Terre Haute, Indiana, Ocober 23, 1871, and arrived in St. Louis with his parents at the age of ten. He graduated from Perkins and Herpel Business College and became a bookkeeper for some prominent firms in St. Louis. Then in 1903 he arrived in Valley Park and rented a small lot on the Meramec, beginning business with a tent, three boats and two canoes. In 1910 he bought a ten acre tract just west of where Highway 141 crosses the Meramec and it became Arnold's Landing. He rented out 40 cottages, had picnic facilities, and a dance pavilion which became a main feature of his operation. At the height of his operation, he had two hundred fifty canoes, several flatboats and rented storage space for four hundred privately owned boats. Labeled as Arnold's Grove, the dance pavilion would later become Schoenberg's and subsequently was purchased by Reno Weggemann, who operated it as the Valley Beach until it was abandoned. The Meramec levy design covered the site of the pavilion.

Just to the east of the old Benton School (later the Valley Park City Hall) was a multistoried structure built for managers of the Plate Glass Factory just after the turn of the century.

In later years, it suffered some neglect and was taken over by Mr. and Mrs. Mott who soon renovated it and operated it as a nursing home for some time.

Another and later nursing home was located off Fern Ridge between Forest Avenue and Meramec Station Road. It was operated for a number of years by Ken Moss. It finally became a facility operated by IHS and outlasted the nursing home function of the building east of the old Benton School/City Hall operated by Moss.

The History Of Valley Park

MEDICINES, MEDICINE MEN AND A MEDICINE WOMAN

In the Dupree Atlas of 1838, referred to earlier, a village of Sulphur Spring is identified along the Meramec River, a part of what is now Valley Park. Another map, this one in 1855, identifies the site as Sinking spring. It was close to the edge of Valley Park. Sulphur Springs Road took its name from the former. What is now left of that road is referred to as Vance Road in Valley Park until it leaves the City and picks up its earlier name of Sulphur Springs Road. Many of the visitors to Valley Park came to the Sulphur Springs area to sample the mineral water. Some came to camp at the site and seek the waters as a cure for whatever might afflict them. Those who did not wish to brave the rigors of camp life could rent a room at Frank Sanders West Point House Saloon and Boarding House. There, they might rent a horse and carriage from the livery stable on Mr. Sanders' wagon yard to transport them to the spring. Entrepreneurs in the health field bottled these waters and sold the product as a sure-cure for dyspepsia, liver diseases, fever and ague, rheumatism and a host of other ailments.

Through The 20th Century

We know from the case of John Doherty that a number of physicians either lived in Valley Park or were available nearby but most residents seldom received professional medical attention. This was true as late as the beginning of the Twentieth Century according to Ruth Van Dover, who arrived in Valley Park in 1899 with her family from Peoria, Illinois. She recalled that when flu or a common cold struck, the preferred remedy was to have the chest rubbed with goose grease. No doubt this could compete with the discomfort of many treatments given in more recent times. Preceding the time the first train ran through Valley Park in 1853 and immediately following, there were exceptions to the reluctance to see a physician since a number of injuries were sustained by railroad workers.

A medical practitioner of the day was B. B. Darling who invented a patent medicine known as "Indian Blood Syrup," billed as the "best remedy known to man." There was no indication as to what it remedied. It claimed that 9,000,000 bottles had been sold since introduction in 1870. If marketed earlier, that number of bottles would have had a better chance of being accurate since many of the railroad workers were stricken with cholera and were trying anything. A number of them simply left their jobs and could not be persuaded to return.

Another physician, one for whom we can record more credentials was Adolph Gaudy. Born in France in 1843 he came to the U. S. in 1864 and arrived in Valley Park in 1868. He attended medical school in France where his father was a physician. He had been an assistant surgeon in the French army. Gaudy held membership in the county and state medical societies, and the American Medical Association. He practiced in Valley Park for over 43 years. Dr. Gaudy lived in Valley Park with a cousin, Caroline Delcourt Mills and her husband Samuel Mills.

A. E. B. Wiggins practiced in Valley Park only a short time and moved away. In 1881 Dr. M. Clay Wyatt set up a medical practice in town and was joined a year later by his son Dr. George Wyatt.

While not a medical practitioner, John B. Marquitz ran a general store in which he sold "pure wines and liquors for medicinal purposes." He was the son of Anton and Lucia Marquitz and brother of William who took part in running the store. There is no record of whether the citizenry made more visits to a physician's office or to the store for medicinal remedies when there was an onset of illness, nor do we have statistics on how many people chose goose grease or other remedies.

J. O. Sturdy came to Valley Park in 1893 and set up a "practice" in the treatment of rheumatism and related ailments. This was on the heals of establishing a saloon. He had a number of patients who swore by his treatments but he had to close the "practice" when it was learned he had no diploma. We do not know if he used another "syrup" in his treatments or some other "medicinal purpose" formula. John Sturdy later held public office in the City and he ran an ad in the September 29, 1917, Valley Park Sun touting his services as a Notary Public and agent for Life, Accident, Fire and Tornado Insurance.

A Boos Publication, The *St. Louis County Directory of 1909*, lists two physicians with a Valley Park address – Joseph C. Gallagher with an office in the Office Trust Building and D. A. Gaudy with an office on Meramec Road (presumably Meramec Station Road).

In the 1920's and beyond, a well-known physician in Valley Park was Dr. Frank P. Knabb who made many house calls throughout the community to examine and treat a number of residents still around after the end of the Twentieth Century. Around the 1930's, Valley Park had something of a pioneer as a medical practitioner in the form of a female physician, Dr. Clara Gebert. She had an office upstairs over Weggemann's grocery store on the corner of Marshall and Meramec Station Road. Her residence, with a unique structural design on Forest Avenue, stood intact at the beginning of the Twenty First Century. An article in the St. Louis Globe-Democrat noted an incident in the life of Dr. Gebert. She and her husband had retired for the night when a phone call came from a family where the birth of a baby was imminent. It was from the Lang home on the banks of the Meramec which had overflowed and isolated the Langs from land. Dr. Gebert's husband got up with her, drove her to the water's edge, where Mr. Lang met her in a boat, and she went by boat to the Lang residence with her satchel. Dr. Gebert took care of the delivery of the baby, phoned her husband who met her at the water's edge where she disembarked from Lang's boat, and the two returned to their residence on Forest Avenue.

During the 1940's, when the State of Missouri began requiring physical exams for high school students to participate in athletic competition, J. M. Cottingham obliged without charge. He had his office in the Village of Twin Oaks, immediately north of Valley Park on Meramec Station Road. A graduate of the Kirksville School of Osteopathy and Surgery, he was a huge man, especially around the waistline. He sometimes employed coarse language. He would sit at his typewriter using a hunt and peck system to record patient information or details of a prescription. An ever present cigarette dangled from his lip and spilled ashes on his ample waist. Anyone present and observing would experience anxiety lest at any moment the doctor's white shirt would erupt in flames although we know of no instance when it did. A young lad had been rolling a barrel by standing on it and moving his feet backward as the barrel rolled. One end of the barrel was open with a jagged edge exposed. Making a miscue, the unlucky youngster slipped over the edge and tore a large hole in the flesh of his inside upper thigh. When brought into the office, Cottingham looked at the wound and said, "Hell, that's nothing. I'll sew that up like your momma sews up a hole in your britches." The boy winced at the first of four injections to deaden the tissue around the perimeter of the wound. "Why are you squirming?" asked Cottingham. "Hell, your dad should be the one flinching. Those shots are five dollars apiece." The doctor then did a superb job of closing the wound as he did in so many other instances with other patients.

During the decade of the sixties, Cottingham's office practice had been turned over to William Burton Gedney, M. D. In spite of the long waits in his office, his numerous patients kept coming. Apparently they appreciated the time he took when he examined and visited with them. His unhurried approach put patients at ease and his reputation as a hospital staff member was unexcelled. He was a graduate of St. Louis University School of Medicine and the son

The History Of Valley Park

of the owner of the Kirkwood Stair Company, which had moved to Valley Park from Kirkwood and located on St. Louis Avenue. In 1998. Gedney turned over his practice to Dr. Pedro Suarez, who, along with Dr. Lorina Shniter, used the office until near the end of that year when the office moved south to a Fenton location.

EDUCATION

Long-time residents mention the existence of private schooling before 1882, but it was in that year that the School District purchased land from George Lyman for thirty five dollars for construction of the first public school. It was located atop Meramec Station Road just south of the intersection with Fern Ridge. Levi Wellington Longnecker started in the small building and his sister, Ruth (Longnecker) Van Dover started in 1902. Ruth Van Dover recalled how the teacher or one of the older boys in class fed a large wood stove in the back of the school room to fight off the winter cold. In 1903 a second building was constructed on the plot and the two buildings were known as the "hill" schools. (That second building was the site of the organizational meeting to establish Valley Park as a City.)

In the earlier days of the hill schools, if a student had to leave the room for a necessity, it involved a visit to an outdoor privy. Water sometimes had to be carried to school in those early days. The hill schools housed grades one through five and by the time Ruth Van Dover was ready for the sixth grade, construction of the Benton School, (3rd Street and Benton) had progressed to where it was ready to receive students at the sixth grade level. Kaecheld, Maud Kinkead, McNaughton, Mary Daily and Brantley are names of teachers who staffed the "hill" school complex. Mary Dailey later became Mary Babke and served as Valley Park Postmaster for many years. Miss McNaughton married Dr. Gallagher, one of the plate glass factory doctors.

At the Benton School, Ann Humphries recalls being taught by Henry Williams as do all who ever attended Benton in its early years. He was tough, she thought, but she learned a lot from him. Many of his students echoed that same appraisal. "What a wonderful teacher he was," said Ruth Van Dover. Former Benton students indicate that there were four rooms in the building but on cold days only two of the rooms were warm enough, so, said long time resident Doris (Jones) Wapelhorst, "…we had to double up. Sometimes after running all the way to school we had no heat at all and were advised to return home." In such instances not all students returned home. Many of them who had to come a considerable distance from farms surrounding Valley Park chose to visit the "hill" school primary class of Miss Kaecheld. There was warmth there from a stove which was now using coal and water was available to use with lunches they had brought. At recess they could go sledding down a nearby snow-covered path, and passing the day in that fashion, avoid the chores which were likely awaiting them at home – a case of youthful ingenuity.

Mrs. Henry Williams (Jessie) also performed teaching duties at Benton School and received praise from Nellie (Rue) Reed, one of her students. The Forrester sisters, who arrived daily as students in a horse and buggy driven by their mother from a farm south of town, later became teachers. Marie Forrester taught four of the children of Nellie Rue who said her children "loved her."

Those students who attended the "hill" schools began transferring to the seventh grade at Benton, as Ruth (Lasley) Heinemann recalled doing. She graduated from Benton's eighth grade around 1914 and commuted by train to St. Louis where she took classes in business, bookkeeping, and business English. She worked in Maplewood as secretary to the Mayor there for a short time before she was married in 1915. Her husband was Charles Heinemann, who served on the School Board in the twenties.

Kathryn McGhee recalled being in a "Tom Thumb" wedding and in another play directed by Mr. Williams. In that other Benton School production she was obliged to kiss another player. She did so but only after much coaxing and cajoling by Mr. Williams who complained about having to pay a royalty which he thought was too high.

The History Of Valley Park

Although few remember him, Professor C. H. Boehn is listed in the Boos publication of 1909 as the Principal of Valley Park Schools.

A growing population in and around Valley Park prompted the Board of Education to construct a new school to house both elementary and high school classes. This school was built on Meramec Station Road at the intersection with Vance Road (Sulpher Springs Road) where the complex is still located. The school opened in 1932. Grades one through six were on the first floor and grades seven through ten were on the second. Enrollees came from the Manchester area and surrounding parts along with students from the Fenton area in addition to Valley Park residents. The Benton School remained open for students in grades one through eight serving the "Newtown" section. There was no Rockwood District (although there was a Eureka High School). Neither was there a Parkway District nor Lindberg District. Around 1939 there was a movement to send all students to Benton for grades one through six and all seventh through twelfth students to the new building. Residents in the older section of town opposed this and the early arrangement remained. A subsequent compromise was to have grades one through six at Benton for the "newtown" section and one through six at the new school for students in the older sector, with grades seven to twelve for all at the new school.

Through The 20th Century

Not too surprisingly, Henry Williams became the Principal of the newly opened Junior-Senior High School. He taught all the social studies classes and students found a remarkable consistency in all his classes in grades seven through twelve. His reference to a cigarette as a coffin nail was the earliest application of that label his students could recall. It was all a no nonsense approach with a zero tolerance for any severe misconduct. Severity was defined by Mr. Williams. In a class reunion, one of his students recalled in commenting to former classmates about a student who had used a forbidden monosylable in class. Said Donald Hart, who made the reference, "…we never saw him again."

Harry Lee Simpson, a member of the first graduating class, said, "That man taught me more about life and living – about things I needed to know – than anyone can imagine."

As he approached the age at which he was eligible to retire, Mr. Williams was still going strong. He stayed on well after that eligibility and continued the admonitions on economics (Be thrifty, save some money, buy savings bonds) along with timely suggestions on preparation of food. Do not peel potatoes and throw away the best of the nutrients. Boil potatoes with the jackets on and get the nutrients which most people throw away. Then there was the matter of doing a job thoroughly which led him to reveal a one-time shortcoming of his own. He told of his father directing him and his brother to dig up potatoes. He announced that the job was done. His father took the hoe, and after a short distance of digging, found a potato. "Now," said his father, "when you have every potato from every row, your job is done, but not before."

He also weaved other lessons into the rich history of the United States and at any time a student might be called to the blackboard to list the conditions following the French and Indian War or the Causes of the Civil War or Wilson's Fourteen Points or any of a host of other historical items which were covered in class. When a student was seated Mr. Williams might mention one of these historical data collections and call on the student by saying, "Give it." or he might pose a question about the times. On one occasion, Mr. Williams mentioned the Great Depression and the foreclosures taking place. He pointed out that when the county judge and sheriff came to the driveway leading back to an Iowan farm that was slated for foreclosure and an auction, there were farmers standing across the entry holding shotguns at the ready and one of the farmers said, "Judge, there ain't gonna be no sale today.""Now," said Williams, "What would you do in that case if you were the judge? "To Ed Corcoran, he said, "Give it."Ed replied, "No sale!" emphatically and elicited a grin and a chuckle from

Mr. Williams. No event was too trivial if it furnished some kind of lesson. He traveled extensively and told of chickens he observed on the plains during a rather heavy windstorm. The chickens had "learned something." They faced the wind and their feathers were held close to their bodies. Otherwise they would have had their feathers ruffled and been blown helter skelter. As he told the story, he partially folded his arms and crouched to imitate the posturing of the chickens. The lesson? Face your problems head on and do not try to run from them or even turn your back on them.

A number of students didn't like Hank as they sometimes called him (but not in his presence). But in reflection, most did like him and no one could deny that he forged a set of lessons that burned a pathway to the brain, imbedded there and dared anyone to dislodge them.

The Sacred Heart School was opened close to the same time that the same name Catholic Church was dedicated July 4, 1908. The Church cost about $40,000 with additional values in the form of gifts for beautiful interior decorations. The Parish School, staffed by Sisters of Notre Dame, opened soon thereafter with 29 pupils and has continued in operation since. Mary Young (formerly Mary Duff) attended Sacred Heart School from September 1910 until 1918. She recalled studying catechism, reading, spelling, geography, history, arithmetic, and writing along with drawing and needlework.

The History Of Valley Park

Lol Halker (formerly Lol Dwyer), who came to Valley Park in 1926 with her parents and siblings, remembered that each grade had between eight and ten students. Two grades shared a classroom which was a common practice in public as well as parochial schools.in those times. Ann Ward started at Sacred Heart in the same year (1926) in the much "older building which was torn down when the new school was built in 1966-67." All of those students remember, along with Virgie (Slezak) Tyrey, who attended in the 40's that "...we walked to school and carried our lunches whether it was raining, snowing, or the sun was shining." Dorothy Cuchetti Kettler recalled that she and two others were the only, members of her graduating class from Sacred Heart High.

In January of 1916, Sacred Heart Church was struck by lightning. While there was damage to the belfry and clock, no fire resulted. The same strike caused darkness throughout the town for about half an hour before power was restored.

Throughout the Thirties, public school and parochial school student bodies and their families came together to attend the public school picnic which would very nearly close down most of the usual activities in town. A passenger train would wait for its human cargo on the Missouri Pacific switch track just east of Meramec Station Road and baskets filled with picnic necessities would be loaded on in preparation for the annual trip to Forest Park Highlands. The Highlands, which would later furnish a site for the Forest Park Community College, was the earlier version of the Six Flags complex with the exception of size and the fact that the stay at the Highlands was not as likely to involve visitors from other parts of the country, even though that was sometimes the case.

The train would begin its eastward journey and gradually pick up speed as it neared the tunnels which remain on the property of the St. Louis County Museum of Transport, established after that section of the track was abandoned. It was always something of a thrill to suddenly find the train engulfed in a semi-darkness with the only illumination coming from the interior lights of the train and then emerge amidst the smoke which had accumulated while the engine was negotiating the tunnels. The train would pull onto a siding south of the Highlands and eager youngsters would charge from the train cars up the incline carrying a portion of the family's picnic supplies to set on a table in the Highlands grounds so as to claim that table as a base of operations for the day. Each of the one day homesteaders would have a number of tickets which were good for free rides on some of the more popular attractions. After spending the day with thrills on the airplane swing, the racing derby (later

The History Of Valley Park

renamed the comet), flying turns (renamed bobsled), and the merry-go-round, along with other rides and consuming the family's picnic fare, the picnickers would return to the train for the ride back to Valley Park. When the train arrived back in town and discharged the revelers, the town which had slept most of the day would resume its more customary routines. The threat of the onset of WWII doomed the train ride to the Highlands for the annual picnic, but those who took part in the ritual remember it as something special. But we have inserted too much of the thirties and forties too soon and need to look at the late teens and roaring twenties in more detail.

Through The 20th Century

EARLY 1900'S

The September 29, 1917, edition of the Valley Park Sun announced the passing of its long time editor, Thomas Edward Ryan. He published near the mid first decade of the Twentieth Century and beyond. He was born in Holly Springs, Misissippi, April 19, 1848, and when Civil War erupted he was too young to enlist but near the close of the war joined a regiment and stayed until the end of the conflict. Taking up printing, he worked at Slossam Brothers, at the corner of Main and Olive, in St. Louis and moved to Valley Park in October 1906 and established the Valley Park Sun. He had been married in Elmo, Texas, in 1877 to Miss Sarah F. Stovall. The couple had eight children of whom seven survived his passing – four sons and three daughters. His funeral service was conducted by Rev. C. C. Berry of the Methodist Church and he was buried in Oakhill Cemetery in Kirkwood.

In that same issue of the Valley Park Sun, two hotel advertisements ran for the Frisco Hotel and the Valley Park Hotel. The former offered permanent guests a room for $7 weekly and the latter offered a spring chicken dinner for 75 cents. Also in that issue was a directory of churches and

The History Of Valley Park

other entities: Sacred Heart Catholic Church, Rev. Father F. S. Recker in charge; Methodist Church, South, Rev. C. C. Berry, Pastor; St. Lukes Episcopal Church on the southeast corner of Fifth and Benton; Evangelical Lutheran-Zions Church with service in German every first and third Sunday of the month and English services every second and fourth Sunday at 2:30 p.m.

Also in the directory were The Business Men's League, A. F. and M. – Valley Park Lodge, Valley Park Camp of Modern Woodmen of America, Valley Park Lodge – Loyal Order of the Moose, and the W.C.T.U – second Friday afternoon of each month.

On the heels of the great flood which wiped out the glass factory and many businesses in town, not many people paid attention to the sign adjacent the Frisco Hotel which read *F. C. Sanguinet, Builder and Contractor*. The Frisco Hotel had water half way to the first floor ceiling. At another gathering place, the A.B.C. Bar on Meramec Station Road by the railroad tracks, there was another sign posted – this one inside the bar, and it read, *Absolutely No Credit*. E. J. Rauscher, proprietor, had closed for the night but the charging Meramec waters had pushed open his door and Sunday morning's rescue crews saw the open door and entered in canoes. There they found a willing host in the proprietor who had been taking stock of his losses, and beer, iced in tubs, made the rounds until Sheriff Bode found out about the situation and arrived to declare the bar closed. He feared that some of the rescuers might not be as competent after one beer too many.

Some residents took to second story porches and some to roof tops from which they yelled for assistance or discharged their firearms to attract the attention of rescuers.

On November 11, 1918, World War I fighting ended and the world had supposedly been made safe for democracy. It was a happy time in Valley Park where the Babka grocery and variety store was located on Marshall Road. Nellie (Rue) Reed recalled that her grandfather bought every horn, drum, whistle or whatever other items were suitable as noisemakers and gave them to children who marched in an impromptu parade to celebrate the armistice.

Not many in Valley Park or elsewhere, realized that we were officially at war with Germany until 1921 because the U. S. refused to ratify the peace treaty with Wilson's Fourteen Points. Minus the Fourteen Points the Senate ratified a treaty in the year noted and the war was officially over. But once the fighting was over, Valley Park, like other parts of the nation, was ready for isolation.

In 1913, Valley Park wage earners and those throughout the nation had to pay a tax based on the income formula

The History Of Valley Park

following the 16th Amendment which had been proposed in 1909. In 1920 Women got to vote for the first time nationwide following adoption of the 20th Amendment. If women in Valley Park followed the national trend, most of them voted for Warren Harding. But of greater immediate impact was another amendment which prohibited intoxicating beverages, the 18th. Near the end of WWI the emphasis on supplying grains for troops afield helped those who opposed "demon rum" in their efforts to stop the production and consumption. There is much to be said for the observation of George James that it "…made it possible for a lot of gangsters to make a lot of money."

In the "Roaring Twenties" Valley Park became a kind of hang-out for questionable elements from the metropolitan area, St. Louis City in particular, and having been a popular resort area for so long, most of the questionable characters knew their way around town. It did impose a burden on the town's reputation, justified or not. There were stories of cock fights and considerable rowdiness although most of this was lost on a majority of the young who never knew about the seemier side of life in the town.

The author, as a pre teen in the late 30's, did witness the presence of slot machines at carnivals sponsored by some of the leading organizations in the community. At the time, gambling by playing slot machines and their presence was illegal.

In a piece of literature titled "Big Mitch" (the nickname for author Mitchell), the author tells of coming to Valley Park from the area west of Rolla, Missouri, and making the scenes of Valley Park hangouts. One mentioned prominently is Hotel Hodnett. "Mitch" was a big boy and the gang he ran with was always pitting him against a favorite of another gang. Mitch usually won out with his six foot, six inch muscular frame. He would later move to California where he became a member of the City Council of Salina.

Hotel Hodnett had an upstairs where rooms were sometimes rented by the hour and such rentals continued until around the mid nineteen hundreds.

Notwithstanding George James's comments about gangsters making a lot of money on prohibition, there were marginal dealers not considered to be gangsters – at least not by the general population. George James told of certain employees at Scullin Steel where he worked. They brought cartons of beer to sell to other employees and no one blinked an eye at the situation. Listening to comments of old timers, there are stories about the milk man delivering certain beverages other than milk into customer's homes.

The History Of Valley Park

In later years, Louise Reichwein, mother of the author's high school classmate, Warren, told the story about her husband, Joe Reichwein, when he was a deputy county sheriff. The feds moved their agents around frequently to lesson the likelihood that they would become too friendly with a local and overlook wrongdoings – like violating the Volstead Act. (The law passed by Congress to enforce the Prohibition Amendment.) One such agent had 'busted" a local owner and operator of a saloon/restaurant for dispensing forbidden beverages. That was Vic Girard. His brother, "Toot" Girard, ran the saloon/restaurant with him. The Girard brothers mother, was a moving force in operation of the business.

A different agent was dispatched to pick up Girard, sentenced to one year, and Deputy Sheriff Joe Reichwein was enlisted to take the agent to Girard. Then Girard was to be escorted by the agent and Deputy Reichwein to Union, Missouri, where the feds rented the county jail to house the overflow of prisoners, since violations were so common and federal prisons could not accommodate all the offenders. Girard was sitting at dinner when the agent and Deputy Reichwein entered. Girard asked the agent if he would like to join him for dinner and the agent accepted. Then, in a bold move, "Toot" Girard asked the agent if he would like something to drink and the answer was yes. Girard and the agent had two or more somethings before they left for the journey to Union. In Eureka, Girard asked the agent if it would be all right to stop at a little place operated by a friend and the agent obliged. They had a few more somethings and resumed their trip – until Pacific. There, Girard noted another friend who operated a little place and wanted to bid him farewell before beginning his sentence in Union. The agent agreed and more somethings were downed. Arriving in Union, Deputy Reichwein had both the prisoner-to-be and the agent by their arms, both of them tottering, and the jailer asked, "Which one of them do I get?" Reichwein said, "You can have them both as far as I am concerned, but this is the one (pointing to Girard) that you want."

One of Vic Girard's contemporary friends went to Union to visit Vic while he was serving his sentence. He got the cell number and went down to the cellblock. He came back to the jailer and announced that the cell door was open and there was no one in the cell. "Oh, I know where he is," said the jailer. "In the morning I unlock the cells so the boys can go down to the pool hall. They come back in the evening for the lockup." Small wonder that prohibition was winked at, especially if one realizes that the Harding administration had a man on duty at the White House to provide selected visitors with something stronger than the pink lemonade or another officially sanctioned beverage. And, perhaps with the cavalier attitudes toward alcoholic beverages and extensive violations, it was understandable that Valley Park, a long time playground for the St. Louis area, would harbor some of the characters who helped in the development of the sometimes unsavory reputation that occurred. Perhaps violation of a national law encourages violations of a number of other laws.

In back of the Gem Theatre, along Marshall Road just to the east of the then Frisco Railroad was a building housing the Valley Park Distillery which ran ads as early as 1881 promoting Deutchlander Whiskey ($2.35 per gallon) and the ads continued in 1917, the year Congress passed the Volstead Act to enforce the 18th Amendment. On January 16, 1920, prohibition went into effect at midnight.

Federal agents were dispatched to destroy alcoholic beverages where these were known to exist and the Valley Park distillery was one of the sites. Agents arrived late in the evening and planned to return the following day after putting a padlock on the door of the distillery. When the agents arrived the following morning to destroy the whiskey, they found the whiskey barrels empty. Locals who worked at the distillery knew exactly where each barrel was located and in the middle of the night entered the crawl space under the distillery with a drill, buckets and a funnel. They drilled up through the floor into each of the barrels and drained them dry. This account came from Bob Vance, who knew many names of the "locals" who took part in thwarting the feds attempts to destroy the illegal beverages.

The man from the City Ice and Supply looked in customer windows at the cards displayed in the 20's, 30's and 40's. Those cards were numbered 25, 50, 75, and 100 in such a way that the upright number on top would indicate the number of pounds of ice to be delivered. This was dependent on which way the card was turned in the customer's window. The ice man had a gunny sack over his shoulder and held the block of ice with large ice tongs, balancing the block of ice on the gunny sack as he entered the customer's home. Kids often hoped for the ice man to chip some small pieces of ice around the bed of the truck when the larger blocks were cut into smaller ones. This furnished a refreshing diversion from the day's usual activities.

In 1929 a real estate development called Pharoah Valley opened and a huge sphinx, approximately 20 feet high, was built with a plot of lots and the development agent's office inside. It was located just east of where the glass factory had been located. The agent was there to greet propective buyers, who stayed away in droves and the project fell flat. It had street names like Palm, Pyramid, Oasis, Cairo, Nile, Kena, and Karnak. Some of those names endured.for years and were still around at the end of the 20th Century.

The History Of Valley Park

THE DIRTY THIRTIES

In October of 1929 would come an economic blow to the economy which devastated the nation and Valley Park had no more chance of avoiding its impact than it had a chance to escape the earlier flooding of the Meramec which, nevertheless furnished a measure of fishing fun into the 30's. This was evident when Charles Heinemann and his brother Harry (sons of Charles and Lillian Heineman) posed with a catfish about as long as the brothers were tall. The "cat" was suspended from a sturdy pole, held over their heads by Charles and Harry.

In those "dirty thirties" jobs were lost with business failures and many were left in serious debt as a result of the depression. The "Roaring Twenties" had ended with a crash and many who had been prospering found themselves in desperate straits. The plight of one time high rollers led to the circulation of a story about a person checking into a hotel room. It was said that the hotel clerk would ask, "Do you want it for sleeping or jumping?"

A grocery store on Third and St. Louis Avenues, owned by the Stearns and Starks, sold bananas for five cents per pound and other groceries were low priced but people didn't have money to buy much of the store's wares. The owners extended and over extended credit and the business failed as did so many others during this unfortunate period in history. A sign posted on the closed grocery store simply read, "Dispossessed." One resident of Valley Park, Bill Villhard, shoveled coal from a railroad car on the siding as part of an effort to maintain some financial stability. A train would pull along the switch track by the side of the Valley Park Elevator building, also known as the Mill, close to 141 about a block north of the Meramec, where its coal car would set until unloaded for the Valley Park Elevator Cooperative.

Leonard Seville lived across Forest Avenue from the Missouri Pacific Railroad and remembers seeing people walking along the rails with a bucket. They picked up coals which had been spilled from the coal cars to take home and use for heating.

Hobos came door to door to ask for a sandwich and more often than not, an understanding resident obliged. The author's mother gave a sandwich to a number of drifters. A fencepost in front of the house had a chalk mark left by the recipient of a sandwich to let one of his unemployed brethren know that this house was one where wayfarers could expect a kindness. The pastor of the church of the author's family was a dinner guest two or three times each week. There seemed to be no explanation for this practice at the time but in later years came the realization that it was just a case of wanting a meal which was so often unaffordable for the pastor day to day.

The Missouri Pacific Railroad opened a new stretch of railway through Valley Park, elevated to put it out of danger of flooding from the Meramec. Executives of the Railroad traveled on the new section on a special train on January 15, 1931, in its initial use. The project cost $4,500,000 for the approximate ten and one half mile stretch west to Eureka. A new passenger station was constructed on elevated pillars to make it level with the tracks. It was just to the east of Highway 141 on the south side of the railroad tracks. This station was razed in the 1980's leaving the pillars in place. An underpass for the elevated tracks was created for Highway 141 with two traffic lanes. Viaducts for underpasses were created for Lake Hill Road at Didian crossing. While the Missouri Pacific seemed to prosper, many individuals did not, and some resorted to burglary or robbery. There was a fall bank robbery of the Meramec Valley Bank. Employees were forced to kneel and the robbers made off with $3,500. They escaped in a car with an Illinois license. West of Valley Park, clubhouses were burglarized and City Marshal James O'Brien interrupted one burglary in progress at 2:00 A. M.

The burglar was jailed because of inability to post a $2,000 bond.

April 21, 1933, a new Lions Club house was dedicated with some 200 members and guests present. Logs for the building came from the forested area along Highwayy 66, dragged by horses or mule teams to the building site where St. Louis Avenue and Marshall Avenue converge to form a wedge near the east end of town. The pay per log being hauled was 25 cents each. The structure was composed of the logs and concrete masonry chinking between the logs. Workers on the project were paid in groceries and other necessities by the Lions International. H. V. Girard was the Lions Club President. Over the years, the Lions Club has been active in furnishing assistance to those in need as was the case during the depression. In addition to helping those in need the Lions provide fun filled activities during the holiday seasons, Christmas and Easter.

For many years, an Easter Egg hunt was sponsored by the Lions Club and at a signal, the hunters rushed to find as many eggs as possible with some of the eggs getting crushed in the hunt. But children loved the event.

In April of 1933 Congress passed and Roosevelt signed into law the *Emergency Conservation Work Agency.* (In 1937 it was extended and officially renamed the *Civilian*

The History Of Valley Park

Conservation Corps). Work camps were set up and usually operated by the War Department. A headquarters was established for an eastern sub-district of the organization in Valley Park under the command of Lt. Colonel H. S. Ramsey who had been a citizen of Valley Park for 6 years. A number of young men in Valley Park took advantage of the opportunity for unmarried and unemployed citizens, ages 17-23 to work on the various projects in which the organization was active. The men were paid $30 per month, half of which was sent home to parents or guardians.

A familiar sight along the streets was the horse and buggy of Mr. Mueller along a paper route where he threw a newspaper in front of each customer's house. When there was a short street or a street with only a few customers, Mr. Mueller would sometimes dismount and deliver three or four newspapers to an adjacent street and find his horse waiting at the end of that street to resume the ride. The horse had become familiar with the route and knew where to meet Mr. Mueller in such instances. Mr. Mueller never had much to say so far as the kids along the way knew. Some of them delighted in grabbing on to the back of his buggy and snitching a ride for whatever distance they could. The ride would end abruptly when Mr. Mueller pulled his buggy whip off the side of his rig and delivered a pop toward the youngster hanging on at the rear. It brings to mind the poem,

Through The 20th Century

"Jest 'Fore Christmas" where kids would try to hitch a ride on the grocery cart, especially the main subject of the poem who owned a clipper sled.

In those thirties, a resident might have read any of three daily newspapers, although the percentage of the population subscribing was minimal. The Post-Dispatch, Globe-Democrat and the Star Times were published daily. The Star-Times was the first to fold (1951) followed by the Globe-Democrat (1986).and the St. Louis Post-Dispatch was left as the only St. Louis daily.

There were other deliveries. Roy Bamber arrived at households with a truck full of bread and pastries. He was a personable fellow and had memorized a slogan which he rattled off frequently: *"Better buy Bamber's better bakery bread for better built bodies, blood, bones, and brains."* Bamber was succeeded by Jake Keller who carried the same products and made the same rounds for some time. A little earlier a resident might have made a trip to a bakery goods outlet at Schaperkoetters at Third and St. Louis. It was immediately east of Third Street across from the Valley Park Trust building on the north side of St. Louis. Both buildings would survive into the 21st Century.

Bamber's and later Jake Keller's deliveries were not the only door to door deliveries. The Slezak brothers-Phil, Tony,

The History Of Valley Park

and younger brother Matt, lived on Inez at the corner of Ravine. They had a truck used to carry and sell vegetables in Valley Park and surrounding areas. Their sister, Virgie, became the wife of Owen Tyrey, and they built their house closer to Ravine Avenue on that same corner where she grew up and where a small truck garden existed and furnished vegetables for the Slezak deliveries.

The Dwyers moved to Valley Park in 1926. There were four sisters and two brother. Lol, Marme, Nancy and Agnes (known to close friends as Wiggie). Lol married Bob Halker, Marme married Bob Vance and Wiggie, the last to marry, became the wife of Wilbur (Rube) Wolfe. The brothers were Jack and Tom Dwyer. Nancy and Agnes tell of the time when some of the girls went riding with some young men from Kirkwood and were gone longer than their dad thought they should be gone. When they returned home, the car was greeted by their dad coming out of the house with a baseball bat. He was not really a violent person but apparently wanted to impress upon the young men that he disapproved of the prolonged accompaniment of his daughters. "It was just an innocent joy ride," noted Nancy and Agnes. Nancy served during WWII as a Wave. At a dance hall it was not uncommon for all patrons to stop what they were doing to watch Dwyer sisters swinging to the music on the dance floor.

Through The 20th Century

On Front Street at Marshall, just west of the Frisco Railroad, Harry Vance ran a tight operation. His bank was one of few that did not need to close following the stock market crash of 1929. Of course, the bank closed of necessity when FDR declared a bank holiday but no one could be found who lost any of their money in Meramec Valley Bank, a claim which not many banks could make in those days. The bank had iron bars and a bullet proof window with a small opening for customer negotiations. It was subsequently remodeled and had only a waist high counter separating the cashier from the customers. After the remodeling, Lawrence Bolte, owner of the market to the west, noted that "Harry" (meaning the cashier, Harry Vance) looked naked sitting there." Emma O'Brien became a cashier and served throughout the tenure of Harry Vance and under the new ownership a number of years later of Bill Jones, Sr.

Toward the east end of town at Fifth and St. Louis on the north side was the Rue family grocery store and gas station. Gasoline was 15 cents a gallon and inside the store a large two layer cake went for thirty-five cents. Pies were a quarter, doughnuts twenty cents a dozen, bread ten cents a loaf, with oysters and mushrooms going for fifteen cents a can.

Another operation toward the east end of town on the south side of Marshall was the East End Garage, owned and operated by William J. Brignole, Sr. He would become Mayor of Valley Park in 1944 when some left over hard times put the City in the awkward position of defaulting on its electric bill. Mayor Brignole paid the bills from his own resources until the City could recover financially. The East End Garage was the site where Charles Mound posed for a picture with members of the baseball team he had sponsored. Fred Mound was the owner of the Gem Threatre (later named the Park Theatre). Dorothy (Cuchetti) Kettler observed that when some of the moviegoers found some evidence of a lack of custodial care in the theatre, they temporarily named it the Germ Theater.

Where St. Louis Avenue begins at its west end, departing from First Street (later named Beckett Memorial Drive) stood Hotel Hodnett, a busy location during the roaring twenties named after the then proprietor. The ownership was taken over by Jimmie Huskisson, who put the facility on the map with his shenanigans of one sort or another. Many ladies were embarrassed there when Jimmie would offer to take their picture. As the camera clicked, a small electrical charge went through the chair where the luckless lady sat and she was photographed in a compromised situation with legs extended outward and up. A lady with modest inclinations would not return to Jimmie's Hotel Hodnett. Not many of the ladies wished to keep the photo as a memento for their visit to Hotel Hodnett. Another feature in the establishment was a large coin on the bar touched by a number of unsuspecting customers. When they did, an electric shock was their reward on touching the coin. Jimmy was great at cracking jokes and he punctuated his punch lines or outcomes of some of his humorous episodes by saying, "Ain't that a mess?" He was the brother of Panama Hattie, well known performer, and his Hotel Hodnett was the subject of a major write-up in a national magazine.

Leonard Seville remembers that he was able to frequent some of the scenes where boys his age were not supposed to be present. He tells the story about an event at the Lions Club of which Jimmie was a member. Jimmie was supposed to be in a match with a professional wrestler who was as muscular as they come. Leonard mentioned that in those days you had to be a business man to be a member of the Lions Club. The event was a fund raiser for the Lions and Jimmie agreed to take part knowing that it was a fix. The pro wrestler was something of a gymnast and acrobat and a good actor. He appeared, flexing his rippling muscles and making those not aware of the fix wonder how Jimmie could last more than a few seconds. Jimmie weighed around eighty pounds, according to Seville (perhaps an exaggeration to emphasize the limitations of Jimmy's chances of competing). So skinny Jimmy emerged from a doorway wearing red, long john underwear with one half of the trap not closed. Jimmy was not known for modesty and his appearance brought howls of laughter from the patrons of the event. After the start, the two "fighters" grappled while those in the audience cheered Jimmie on. It went on until the professional wrestler made a kind of acrobatic flip move which gave the appearance that Jimmie had thrown him to the floor. Jimmie landed on top of the would be fallen foe and appeared to beat him unmercifully and the crowd went wild with cheers and applause. Of course the trap door was still open, much to the amusement of the raucous crowd. In the end, the wrestler and Jimmie clasped hands and held them up over their heads and the crowd erupted with even more applause. We have no record of how much the paid event enhanced the Lions treasury.

From early morning until midnight in the thirties and forties, there was bus service which ran along Meramec Station south to Marshall, east on Marshall then left to St. Louis Avenue and along St. Louis Avenue to the White Mineral Springs swimming pool complex (across St. Louis from the Lions Club property) where it turned around and waited a short while before reversing its path through the City. The route went through Kirkwood and on to Maplewood, with fare in the later thirties of fifteen cents to Kirkwood and twenty-five cents to Maplewood.

Through The 20th Century

On Marshall Avenue, just west of Meramec Valley Bank (toward 141) was a building materials yard just before Cuchetti's Market, a small grocery operation. On to the west of Cuchetti's was Komotos dry goods and shoe repair store. In the thirties, with the economy sour, nearly everyone had shoes half-soled or sewed where needed so as to get maximum wear. Mr. Komotos was a master in the art of shoe repair. Next to the west on Marshall was a small building which housed a barber shop operated by Jim Day. Mr. Day owned a house atop the hill on Jefferson Avenue (just north of what would later become Jefflyn Ave). The lot was a large one and had two or three peach trees in its southwest corner. Youngsters often climbed the fence at night to help themselves to a ripened peach in season. Day's barber shop was also occupied at one time by barber Joe Bim and later by barber "Nappy" Knapheide and Roe Melugin. It's last use was as a dry goods store operated by Irene Duff.

Continuing west was the Kroger Grocery Store. Wayne Emmekus was manager of the Kroger store. One more stop to the west was the grocery store of L. J. Weggemann, with the upstairs furnishing office space for Clara M. Gebert, M.D. That Kroger Grocery Store later became Bolte's I.G.A. Grocery. The store along with the Weggemann Grocery building (It had later become Meningers Grocery) was razed to make way for the new three lanes entry and three lanes exit along with the new bridge. Marshall Avenue formed a T Junction with Highway 141 and on the west side of 141, the Rexall Drug Store was located. It was owned by a man named Krummenacher and became more memorable to the young for its soda fountain and milk shakes than for the various drugs and incidentals. The pharmacist there was Earl Whitehead. The operation was later taken over by Doug and Alice Eadie with Doug serving as the pharmacist. The Eadies had an approximate ten acre tract along what was to become the extension of Big Bend westward from 141 just to the north of the Valley Park city limits. On one occasion, the Eadie's gave a party for officials of the City in the 1960's. After some refreshments, the group began feeling a bit frisky and one of those present was tossed into the Eadie's swimming pool fully clothed.

Back to the thirties, on the south side of Marshall, almost directly across from Krogers, was O'Brien's Buffet and Tavern, a favorite neighborhood gathering place and on the southeast corner of Marshall and 141 was the White Front Restaurant. The latter would be razed later in favor of a laundromat until it made way for the new bridge and new highway into town. If you went north from 141 and Marshall, you passed under the Missouri Pacific viaduct to Forest Avenue (formerly Dougherty Ferry Road) and on that north easterly corner was Dan Wolf's garage where Forest wedged into 141. Next to the north was Wolf's Department Store (later named American Brokerage). A little farther north and across from the intersection of 141 with Vance Road was the Union Electric Company building. It was not an imposing structure and a long time employee of the utility was John Goree who managed the operation. If you had a light bulb which had burned out, you could take it to Goree and he would provide you with a new bulb, no charge. UE would discontinue that practice in favor of making another dollar or two on the sale of light bulbs. People would not go long without replacing a light bulb even though a cost was involved. The sale of light bulbs became a standard retail operation and has remained so. Electric Companies have found it to their advantage to focus on electricity only services.

On the north side of Vance at 141, in a building which still stood at the end of the Twentieth Century, was Henlon's Gas Station and Garage. Warren Henlon was Mr. Shell Petroleum in Valley Park. He also repaired autos as part of the operation. The building later became the site of the Valley Park Bottling Works, under George Hollman with its Virginia Dare soda the main product. It's next use was for a restaurant operation, the Coffee Pot, where LaVerne Ford engaged in conversation with students from the Valley Park Schools, located adjacent to the restaurant. That property

The History Of Valley Park

would be purchased later by Valley Park Schools to house the Dennis Lea Childhood Learning Center. On the southwest corner of the same intersection began a row of buildings which trailed down to the site immediately across the street from Dan Wolf's garage. There was Joe Hertweck's Tavern. Hertweck's and O'Brien's were well patronized. After all, prohibition was over and the alcoholic based beverages could flow freely, and legally.

Hertweck eventually moved north to the southwest corner of 141 and Vance where he continued his operation. The building he vacated became a temporary home of the Church of the Nazarene until vacated in favor of a new building where Main Street turns west and approaches the intersection with Jefferson. By the end of the Century, the Christian Science Church had taken over the one time Church of the Nazarene property. At the old and new location for Hertweck's, it was a common sight to see a patron carrying a bucket of beer which Joe had filled, away from the tavern to be consumed elsewhere, presumably at the patron's home. Youngsters frequently entered Hertweck's for purchase of a twelve ounce bottle of Pepsi Cola, perhaps subliminally persuaded by a commercial which filled the radio air waves:. *'Pepsi Cola hit's the spot. Twelve full ounces, that's a lot. Twice as much for your nickel too. Pepsi Cola is the drink for you. Nickle, nickle, nickle, nickle, ra da ta da."* The ending was punctuated by the sound of a sudden rush of air when a cap is popped off a soda bottle.

Another building almost immediately across from Dan Wolfe's garage was a two-story structure which Fairy May (Steele) Hollerich remembers as an early residence of her family. She and her brothers patronized a little store close by the railroad tracks. Sometimes penny candies went on sale three for a penny and she and her brothers came away with three licorice sticks having received a supposed rare bargain. "We felt so grown up," she said. "When mother would let us walk down the street and select our own candies." She remembers a Sunday morning event when they heard the train (whistle) blowing and blowing and the screech of the train's brakes. "We all wanted to see what happened. My mother told us children not to go any farther than the front yard. Suddenly people were screaming and crying. People poured out of the train. I didn't know what had happened. I just stood and watched the mob of people. Tears streamed down my cheeks and I felt sad. Much later I learned that a young couple had committed suicide by stepping in front of the oncoming train. It was said that their parents would not agree to their marrying." Fairy May was the youngest of six siblings – Louis, Walter, Norman, Jack, and Violet.

In the twenties, a young man moved to Valley Park from his birthplace in Arnett, Oklahoma, and posed for a picture

The History Of Valley Park

near his model T Ford taxi. He often picked up fares at the Missouri Pacific railroad station. One of his fares was Violet Clark from Cape Girardeau and the two were married July 29, 1924, and rented quarters in that two story building across from Dan Wolf's garage. That taxi driver was Fairy May's dad, Roy Steele. He gave up his taxi service and took a job with Price Varnish where he worked until retirement. He organized a baseball team for young boys and took the members to different locales to meet opponents. The team was called the Valley Park Amateurs and was one of a somewhat organized competition for many youngsters in Valley Park, including the author.

Loren Hewitt, VPHS Class of '39, remembers when he was hired to chase down foul balls during the days when Jess Hill managed a baseball team in Valley Park. The home plate was close to Benton Street at the site where the Third Street playground was later located. Loren recalls getting fifteen cents for getting the foul balls back to the diamond site. On one occasion he chased a hard hit foul ball all the way across St. Louis Avenue to Marshall. Loren echoed Steve Hildebrand's assessment of Valley Park as "...the best place for a kid to grow up at that time."

Not a large percentage of the townfolk had a radio and the subscription to a newspaper was similarly small. Ray Pritchett, a long time resident, recalls an event on Benton

Street in the thirties. It got very dark. "People were out on the street wandering to and fro," he said. "I didn't understand and wondered why some people were praying and hoping it wasn't the end of the world. I was scared too and then one of the older guys told me it was nothing to worry about." This was, of course, a case of a number of people not having access to radio or newspapers and being unaware of such a thing as a total eclipse.

Steve Hildebrand remembers the Gem Theatre where he spent many Sunday afternoons watching Hopalong Cassidy movies.

There was the time Steve caught a three pound bass and marched home with it, accompanied by Ed and Fred Dial, twins, who had cane poles like Steve's and often fished the rapids just above the wagon bridge (first used for wagon crossings, the bridge retained that name for many years). Steve had a number of admirers on his route home and remembers it as a real high. The first car Steve ever saw that he "knew the name of" was a Packard owned by L. J. Weggenmann, who owned that grocery store on the corner of 141 and Marshall Avenue. Steve's brother John worked for the Frisco Railroad as did his father and Uncle Charlie, engineers or firemen. Steve lived in a house on Quinwood and remembers the Lochaas family (Rev. Lochaas was Pastor of the Lutheran Church) moving into a house nearby along

The History Of Valley Park

Meramec Station Road across from the Lutheran Church. He also remembered when Gus Schneedle built along the street where he lived and the Berkles family moved in across the street from him.

Steve became a detective on the Clayton Police force and later retired to Florida. He referred to Valley Park as the "best place for a kid to grow up at that time." He remembers taking part in the recruitment of a VPHS graduate, Dale Curtis, for the Clayton Police. He said, "I told Chief Browser, just hire him. You can't do any better, and he did." Steve was pleased to learn that Dale later became the Chief of Police in Webster Groves.

One of the radio heroes of choice in the thirties was "Tom Mix – and his Ralston Straight Shooters." Tom Mix was extensively marketed with secret codes for use with rings, obtainable for a mailed in Ralston cereal box top with some coins. There were sweaters with Tom Mix emblazoned across the front. Of course the marketing could not be complete without a jingle at the beginning of each radio show. *"When it's round up time at breakfast, then it really is a treat. That rich full flavored Ralston made of golden western wheat. Once you try it you'll sure to buy it for it's really swell to eat. Jane and Jimmie too, say it's best for you. Hot Ralston can't be beat."* Jane and Jimmie were prominent characters on the Tom Mix show. In an effort not to be outdone, "Wheaties – Breakfast of Champions," presented "Jack Armstrong, the All American Boy." The favored embellishment here was a long chant announcing the program and then telling the audience why Wheaties should be the breakfast of choice. Another program was prefaced with an identification of the Lone Ranger and then a shouted request, "Return with us now to those thrilling days of yesteryear. From out of the past come the hoof beats of the great horse Silver. The Lone Ranger rides again" Next, the listeners heard the Lone Ranger urging his steed onward, followed by his Indian friend Tonto's admonition to his own mount, "Gettum up Scout." The youngsters in Valley Park were tuned in to these and other radio heroes, as we suspect youngsters in other communities were too.

On Saturdays during the school year in warmer weather weekends and any time during the summer, young boys found enjoyment in fishing and/or swimming in Fish Pot or Grand Glaize Creek. The latter was at the east end of town and the former at the west end. Both emptied into the Meramec and that body of water sometimes furnished a locale for swimming or fishing as well. A big favorite in Fish Pot was the hole users had named the "ice box" because of the springs which bubbled up from its floor.

Some of the older boys obtained a lengthy half-inch steel cable and clamps with nuts and bolts and fashioned a line

The History Of Valley Park

from an elevated part of a tree trunk on one side of the bank downstream from the "ice box." The other end was attached near the base of a tree on the opposite side of the creek. There were sections of tires placed so as not to damage the trunks of either tree where the cable wrapped around it. A steel pipe was fixed on the steel cable. Boys amused themselves by climbing up the tree with the higher attachment of the cable and hanging on to the pipe, shooting to the other side of the creek. The next rider would catch the thrown pipe back at the start and take his turn with a quick glide. Some folded rags were put around the pipe after a few rides when the pipe got too hot to hold after repeated trips.

T. W. McNeese, a former owner of Webb's restaurant in Valley Park, had moved to Sherman, Missouri, to the west and an employee of his was Ray Woods. Ray was something of a daredevil. When the Missouri Pacific built a new bridge across the Meramec at Sherman, Ray dove off the bridge into what some said was only about five feet of water. Valley Park residents joined Sherman, Eureka, and Castlewood in making this a topic of discussion. In Sherman, they took up a collection of an estimated $20 to get Ray to perform the feat again, and he did. People in Valley Park donated a collective $50 to get Ray to dive from the 141 Bridge into the Meramec and he did in the thirties, a head first dive as he had done in Sherman. Continuing with his stunts, Ray went to California where the new Golden Gate bridge was completed in 1947. There he made a dive from that bridge but made some unlucky turns in mid air and landed on his back which was broken. He was crippled from the waist down the rest of his life but oversaw the construction of a swimming pool in Castlewood which was frequented by swimmers from Valley Park. Wintering in Florida around 1960 and on an outing in the Gulf of Mexico, in spite of the fact that he remained a powerful swimmer because of tremendous upper body strength, he had a boating accident and was drowned. Marty Weisenburg gave the Ray Woods story account as he remembered it.

Leaving the digression into the sixties and coming back to the thirties, for those who could scrape up the fare and some extra change for refreshments, there was the St. Louis Cardinals and St. Louis Browns "Knothole Gang." This involved free admission to the games with seating down the left field line. Kids could catch a bus in Valley Park, ride to Kirkwood and there board a street car which turned around at the "loop" just east of the Marine Hospital (Later St. Joseph Hospital). A "transfer" enabled the riders to get off at Grand Avenue and catch a street car north to Dodier where Sportsman Park was located. The Cardinals usually did well in those days. And the Browns? Well, they played too. St. Louis, a shoe manufacturing center at the time, was often said to be first in shoes, first in booze, and last in the American League. In later years, no parent would even think of letting their children make such a trip by themselves, an unfortunate product of changing times.

But continuing with the thirties. The Tom Thumb wedding presentations still delighted patrons at the Benton School and at a play rehearsal, boys and girls were still feeling squeamish about kissing or even pretending to kiss a member of the opposite gender. We know the names of all four who participated in one of the Tom Thumb weddings – William Rue, Shirley Rittenhouse, Dorothy Rue, and Clyde Parker.

In 1931, voters approved a $60,000 bond issue by a 370-73 vote and the following year the Valley Park High school opened its doors at the site which was to become its permanent location. The President of the Board of Education, Charles Scholl, inserted a time capsule in the cornerstone at the northeast corner of the building. The first graduating class had eight members: Mildred Heiss, Helen Dilling, Lillian Heinemann, Bob Bernhardt, Myrtle Palmer, Bill Underwood, Doris Freeman, and Kenneth Shotwell. Mr. Stanley Ellis was the class sponsor. The last class to graduate in the thirties (1939) had 18 members with only two females, a considerable gender switch from the first commencement. When that class of of '39 posed for a picture in 1935 there were 31 members in all including 9 females. A member of that Class of '39, Franklin Booth, became a surgeon in the Chicago area and practiced there until retirement. Others in that class were: Ed Belt who became the President of his own company, Belt Electric, which contracted area wide in metro St. Louis. There was Wilson Rose who for some time was owner and operator of a service station just across 141 from and a little south of the high school building, Arden Hawkins, who operated a service station south of the Meramec along 141 and Jim Curtis, better known as Ray Curtis, who became the owner of a painting decorating company and worked in many of the finest homes in the St. Louis area. His company did the painting/decoration refurbishing of the Fox Theatre in St. Louis. Loren Hewitt, a community leader, was also a member of that class.

John Boly, in the mid 1930's, had become an expert marksman and headed up a Rifle and Revolver Club which met on his property where Main Street ends and Francis Avenue turns north. He had established a range on his property with his targets consisting of a suspended piece of metal behind another piece with a bulls eye cut-out. When a bullet went through the bulls eye, the suspended metal gave out a loud ping to let the shooter know he had scored. Boly was also a friend of youngsters on their way to Fish

The History Of Valley Park

Pot Creek and to a favorite fishing or swimming hole. He often joked with the young folks who thought him to be a very private person until after an encounter with him. John Boly's brother Dave lived in a little house near the entry of the driveway that led from the intersection of Francis and Main Street to the more distant house from the street front in which John lived.

There was no kindergarten in the 1930's and the author remembers his first grade teacher, Una Moore, who later became Mrs. Steigerwald. That disappointed me because I had decided I would marry her when I got older. She had an interesting method of punishment for the boys who were guilty of misconduct. The boy had to sit on her lap and hold a doll. I received such a punishment for an offense I don't remember, and curled up on her lap and went to sleep. It was the last time she employed that tactic. Another of my best remembered teachers was Maxine Vancil, who later became Mrs. Harry Shanight. She discovered me reading a poem which was not the assigned in-class reading in the fourth grade. Well ahead of her time, she did not reprimand me but suggested to the class that they listen "…while Kennard reads a poem he likes." In retrospect the poem seems a bit of hokum but it impressed me for some reason. Her respect for my choice burned the words into my memory and I still remember them *"Bill Peters was a hustler from*

Independence town. He waren't no college scholar, nor a man of great renown, but Bill had a way of doing things and doing 'em up brown. Bill druv the Indepence Stage along the Smokey Hill and I recon if he'd had good luck he be a drivin' still. But he chanced one day to run agin a bullet made of lead which was harder than he bargained for and now poor Bill is dead. And when they brung his body home, a barrel of tears was shed." Like I said, a bit hokey but memorable.

In the fifth grade and again in the sixth grade, both of which Mr. Arthur Steigerwald taught, Friday afternoon was story time, courtesy of a reading by the teacher. He was a brother of Lee H. Simpson, one of the earlier prominent citizens of Valley Park.

Steigerwald began teaching after being a proprietor of a soft drink parlor and a partner with Simpson in the garage business. He was born September 3, 1895, in St. Louis and graduated from St. Mary's College in Kansas. Early in 1918 he had entered the U. S. Army and was discharged in December of the same year.

Those Friday afternoon readings included *Tom Sawyer*, *Huckleberry Finn*, and *Lad a Dog*. Mr. Steigerwald was an accomplished violinist and became the music man for the Junior Senior High School. He gave lessons in his home and in those days students didn't have the money (1930's) to pay for lessons. They cut the lawn and did other chores around the house in exchange for lessons. The girls helped Mrs. Steigerwald with dishes or housecleaning chores. The pair moved to Hawaii and Una Steigerwald would witness the attack on Pearl Harbor in the next decade. Arthur Steigerwald was the brother of Elizabeth M. Steigerwald (born in Knob Lick, Missouri, November 4, 1893) who married Lee Simpson, already mentioned.

That portion of Valley Park which had been built to house managers or other key personnel in the glass factory had indoor plumbing in most cases. The older areas, including the portion on the hillsides, had no inside bathrooms except in a few cases where an old cistern was utilized as a septic tank. In fact, where the sewer system existed, there was no treatment and the absence of sewers throughout the town and no sewage treatment where sewers did exist was a long-time impediment to growth. An outhouse, or privy, was the most common solution in households away from the newtown area. The outhouse or privy was located at the back of a lot and was too far away in the winter and too close in the summer. In milder weather, a lot of time in the outhouse was spent reading an old Sears Roebuck catalog before a page or two was employed for some other usage.

Through The 20th Century

In 1936 a flyer from the Valley Park Police Department circulated announcing a Thanksgiving Ball at the Fenton Farmers Club. A first floor show was to begin at 10:30 p.m. and a second at 1:30 a.m. The Valley Park Chief of Police was Richard H. James and this event was billed as the third annual of such events to provide an emergency relief fund for Valley Park Police. There were to be 20 floor shows and a 10 piece orchestra. This annual activity continued in one form or another until the 1970's.

In the later part of the 30's decade, five lads explored an old house owned by George Petty and located on what was then just outside of town. It was above the second spring near Fishpot Creek and had been vacant and run down for some time. The five entered the house and were in the upstairs when they heard a noise downstairs. Running down, they stopped short of the front door where owner George Petty stood blocking the doorway. The owner demanded to know what the boys were doing there and what business they had being there. Of course, there was no suitable explanation. Petty marched each of the five down to the town Marshal, Richard "Dick" James. The author was one of the five. We were crowded into the back of the Marshal's car and driven around town while the Marshal speculated loudly about taking us off to jail. Then we were taken one by one to our parents and told of our deed. Our parents were told

The History Of Valley Park

that about the only thing to do was to throw all of us in jail. George Petty sat in the front of the car silent while we rode around town thinking we would be imprisoned for life. The Marshal extracted a promise from each of us that we would not repeat the deed in exchange for a decision not to throw us in jail. We were finally deposited in each of our homes. We did not enter Petty's house again.

THE FORTIES

Wendall Wilkie challenged FDR for the presidency in 1940 and FDR coasted to a victory amidst an escalation of a war raging in Europe. In a relatively short time, the U. S. would be involved in World War.

May 2, 1941, the Board of Aldermen received a complaint from two or three citizens about hogs being raised in the City. The Board took note of the complaint but indicated that the complaint would need to be in writing and identify owners of hogs before the City could take any action.

On December 5, 1941, the Board of Aldermen, on a motion by Alderman Weggeman and a second by Alderman Smith, voted unanimously to purchase Christmas lights and decorations. The second monthly meeting was cancelled and the Board, along with the rest of the citizenry and indeed, the rest of the country, were unprepared for the events that followed before the end of the year. Our increasing troubles with Japan were given little attention in Valley Park as was the case elsewhere. On December 6, 1941, the top tune on the Hit Parade was *"Tonight We Love."* The next day, Sunday morning, a housewife, Kathryn McGhee, came out of her house on Pyramid at Kena and announced to her visiting young brother playing in the yard that Japan had bombed Pearl Harbor and we were at war. The next day, Monday, December 8, the entire student body of Valley Park Jr.-Sr. High was called to an assembly in the high school auditorium to listen to a radio address by President FDR. He told of the "dastardly" attack and pledged that we would "…win the inevitable triumph, so help us God." The President assured us that minimal damage had been done, a misrepresentation of fact as we would learn later. Roosevelt declared December 7 a day which will live in infamy.

The importance of the event became more meaningful as names of recent graduates who were casualties of the war came to the attention of students and the larger community. Joseph Wallach, killed in action. Charles Cross, killed in action. Wallace Thomas, prisoner of war in Germany. (Germany and the U. S. were at war shortly after Pearl Harbor). In a school where everyone knew everyone else, even one name in the mentioned categories made the war real. Bobby Thomas, younger brother of Wallace, dropped out of school to join the navy and Jack Van Dover dropped out to join the army. Both would return in the later forties and graduate with the class of '47. (In 1997 when that class held its 50th reunion, the two were awarded Outstanding Citizen citations from the then Gov. Mel Carnahan, for their willingness to serve at an early age and for determining to complete high school education after the war).

Fairy May (Steele) Hollerrich and some classmates are not sure what the occasion was for a party given by Miss Zeiser. Was it for the drama class or what? Fairy May did remember that Don Goree came by wearing his navy uniform and taught the group a new song, Mares Eat Oats. She questioned the spelling of the title and the rest of the song and there could be a number of ways to spell it…Mares eat oats and does eat oats and little lambs eat ivy, kiddle (cattle) eat ivy too, wouldn't you?

Beginning WWII, the bombing of Pearl Harbor was witnessed by John Laretto and Una (Moore) Steigerwald. She had married Arthur Steigerwald and the two had moved to Hawaii (mentioned earlier), Harold Boly, Melvin Brinley, Leroy Ford and Paul Mitchell survived the Bataan Death March. In a stroke of irony, Harold Boly was killed by "friendly fire" while on a Japanese POW transport ship under attack by U. S. aircraft. Lloyd Ford, Jr. took part in the invasion of Iwo Jima in which Joseph Wallach, Jr., lost his life. Elmer Brown and Aubrey Slavens of the U. S. Army and Wallace Thomas, AF, (mentioned earlier) were German prisoners of war. Burel Thomas, younger brother of Wallace, tells of Wallace's pet cat, which gave a measure of company until one morning it was missing – except for its skeletal remains. A rational explanation was that, with the meager rations received by prisoners, someone had killed and eaten his cat.

Many in the high school population were enlisted to assist in enrolling citizens in something called rationing. How many canned goods do you have on hand? How many are in your family? Depending on the answer to these and other questions, a book of stamps was given to each applicant. With the war in the Pacific area, a major supply of tin was interrupted and the supply that was available had to go primarily for military needs. Therefor, food in cans had to be rationed. The stamp books were issued by the Office of Price Administration, an emergency organization set up by the federal government. The books had various colored stamps and could be used for various short supply items.

Some stamps had a shaft of wheat and such stamps entitled the bearer to buy a loaf of bread. Just as throughout the nation, most auto owners in Valley Park had an "A" card which indicated entitlement to a limited amount of gasoline. If you were a farmer you could get a "T" card with the right of more extensive purchases of gasoline with the reasoning that farming should have priority to supply the food needed for our military personnel. At the local Rexall Drug Store you could only buy a tube of toothpaste if you had an empty tube of similar size to turn in for exchange.

Now and then a consumer could get an extra of one thing or another because of an unexpected increase in supply but even then a stamp had to be surrendered. The government would announce the improved supply and which stamp should be used. This was usually a stamp labeled as a "spare" one. There were rumors of black market activity (merchants selling without stamps and some purchasers reselling at inflated prices to those who wanted to buy without surrendering stamps).

The war bond campaign hit Valley Park like it did elsewhere. Saving stamps could be purchased until a book was full and could be surrendered for a bond. Anna Mae (Keller) Bausch remembers buying stamps at school where sales campaigns often took place. She recalled a Four Freedoms play at Valley Park High. Wanda Messerla had a job at Woodenware Products and remembers buying savings stamps each Friday and putting them in her book to be traded for a bond when full. Wanda and some of her girl friends formed a KRAZY KORNY KITTY KAT KLUB and the loose knit organization met by the baseball field at lunch time. We have no knowledge of the agenda or the minutes of meetings and it is doubtful that any existed. Wanda also recalled that the class of '44 was saddened by a tragic auto accident involving Harrison Gibbs, Bob Van Dover, and

The History Of Valley Park

Lorraine Weggenmann. The latter two were killed in the mishap.

Donald Hendrickson and Therion "Wimpy" Winfrey served aboard the Yorktown carrier and Winfrey was later on the battleship Missouri, witnessing the signatures ending the war with Japan. The Silver Star was awarded Jack George and Glenn Longworth, U. S. Army, and as an indication of how small the world was becoming, a girl working on her father's farm in Japan felt the tremors and aftershock of the first atomic bomb and later became a war bride and grandmother of VPHS student Tim Siebe. Along with classmates, Tim interviewed a large number of long time residents of Valley Park in 1980 for publication of insights into local history. This was under the guidance of Eileen Sherrill (VPHS teacher) who later guided another publication commerating the 50th anniversary of the end of WWII, including names of service men and women from the Korean and Viet Nam conflicts along with the much earlier WWI. Sherill brought local history alive at VPHS. She continuously encouraged students to find out more about local history, a great stepping stone to a study of broadened history.

Another small world story is that of Arthur Smith, AF, stationed in England. He had not seen his brother Richard "Hoot" Smith for two years. Richard was the sole survivor of his tank crew, knocked out during the Battle of the Bulge. He was sent to a hospital in England where Art visited with him.

Back on the home front, Grace's Restaurant was a favorite hangout for the high school crowd. It was located where St. Louis Avenue begins at its west end. It was Gus's Restaurant until the Palmers took it over and renamed it Grace's Restaurant. Grace and Clarence Palmer operated the business and exchanged conversation with the teens who came there for a hamburger (or two), played the juke box or played the pin ball machine or all of the above. Glenn Moon and Jim Wideman were the pinball experts. At times, some of the railroad workers stopped by when their jobs brought them into town and service men on leave also patronized the restaurant. In the summer, Grace's was the meeting place for those who were going to take a joy ride with one of the crowd lucky enough to have an auto or access to one. The Reichold Chemical (It had been Price Varnish then Archer Daniels and Ashland) plant and its predecessor plant has taken over the property where Grace's restaurant stood after a similar takeover of the Park Theatre (one time Gem Theatre) which was just to the east of Grace's.

Shirley (Scholl) Nappier recalled her years in "…my wonderful home on Fern Ridge" with birthday parties in the back yard hosting playmates and cousins. She expressed understandable pride in her father who was the first President of the Board of Education and her mother who was the first PTA President. School teachers roomed with her family from time to time. There was an occasion when she was to perform by singing "The Beautiful Lady in Blue" in a talent show but instead ran off the stage to the disappointment of her sister who had worked with Shirley, rehearsing to prepare for the performance. Her mother, Ethel, knitted scarves and sweaters for the military and went to work in the Cotton Factory as one of the replacements for men who had gone off to war. The Cotton Factory, officially called the Absorbent Cotton Company of America, was given an "E" for excellence, an award by which the government recognized a significant contribution to the WWII effort.

Shirley's dad was born on Gen. Harney's farm near Antire Road, southwest of Valley Park. His first home in Valley Park was on Benton Street and the 1915 flood which devastated most of "Newtown" prompted a move to the Fern Ridge address. He was a skilled pianist, playing by ear and mastering a song when he heard it. He developed this talent while in school at Cape Girardeau and neighbors often gathered in summer on the Scholl front steps on Fern Ridge to hear him play and sing.

Shirley's grandfather, George Thomas Scholl was the Scholl in the Sargent and Scholl Livery Stable, an early business venture in Valley Park. George Thomas Scholl was one of Quantrill's guerilla band and Shirley inherited a pistol with Quantrill's name engraved on the handle, a gift from Quantrill to her grandfather.

Among Shirley's fondest recollections are friends she had including Joan Holman, Bonnie Jones, Jeannie Workman, Ginny Komotos and Mary Ellen Dall. Her neighbor, Margie Dunn Haddock, furnished humor – "…kept me laughing constantly." Margie drove her father, Dr. Dunn, on his calls at the early age of 12. Shirley observed that the Catholics were patients of Dr. Dunn and the Protestants were patients of Dr. Knabb. A sad chapter unfolded after she received a letter from Charles Cross and learned on the day she received the letter, he had been killed in action in WWII.

The aftermath of Shirley's graduation night was a bit disappointing. "I remember graduation night was so dull, no dates available. I went to the Parkmoor on Clayton Road with Pat Burdett. She had a car – I didn't." But most of those years were pleasant – returning servicemen, the "Friday and Saturday nights at Valley Beach on the Meramec, meeting new people from all over St. Louis County who were drawn by the big band and dance hall." She met her husband through Ginny Komotos who had been dating his friend and neighbor from Rock Hill.

The History Of Valley Park

A poem written by Shirley's father in 1940, expresses his feelings about the community of which he and his family became a vital part:

"I stopped off, I was put off" is the correct remark,
At a little town named Valley Park.
"A Tank Town" so called on the map
Between Keyes Summit and Ranken Gap.
The sun shone brightly on this little town
So, of course, I had to loiter 'round.
Here was beauty in a setting rare –
A valley wide, hills towering there.
To shield the dawn, to withhold the Sun.
To encircle the sunset when day is done.
Artists all these years have missed
The valley by God and nature kissed.
Redbuds here and sumachs there,
Gossipy sycamores with hoary hair,
Maples tall, silver and red,
Cast color on the elms, still green.
Firebushes flaming by a cottage door,
The Meramec passing with a friendly roar.
Cattle grazing in meadows along the brink,
Lazily strolling down to drink.
Sinking in muddy freshness to their knees
Then strolling back to lie under cottonwood trees.

Up the river a fisherman with a casting rod
Is putting his faith in luck and God.
The railroad's whistle and trains rush by.
They never stop for such as I.
Then one thinks, "Why should they stop for me?"
I will never leave this great valley
Until I find the friends who surely live here.
So I will stay on until I've lost all fear.
I will become a fixture, a part of this sod
In this valley of beauty and so close to God.

Harry Hiscox lived on the other side of Boyd Avenue from our house and across the street from Richard Hildebrand. The three of us would hang out and engage in typical boyhood pursuits. Richard's mom was expert in home made bread and Harry and I often persuaded Richard to go in and beg for a slice, buttered of course. Being the gracious person she was, she would always send out three slices. Harry's mom and dad loved Meramec State Park and in the summers would take their trailer to a camp site on the Meramec River bank. The trailer was fitted with a tent with side flaps attached and a mattress fitted to the inside of the trailer furnished their sleeping quarters. They also had a motor boat. Harry and I were permitted to stay at the park for an entire month while still junior high school age. We had a tent and his parents would come out for two weekends

The History Of Valley Park

while we were there and then stay for two weeks when Elmer Hiscox had his vacation. The rangers would bring a load of firewood by each evening and Harry and I would hide it so that another load would be delivered the following day. In this way, we would accumulate enough wood to build a huge bonfire. In later years, the campers had to go to the storage area and pick up wood for campfires and the no fee for camping was abolished

Those were memorable times and we were fortunate to make a good catch of catfish every night on limb lines baited with soap. We always managed a good supply for Harry's dad, Elmer, and his mom, Stella, to empty our ice chest and take home with them except enough to supply meals for us at the campsite. All of us were sometimes joined by Harry's older brother Raymond and his wife Virginia.

Those days are long gone now with fees (noted) for using a campsite and limited time for occupancy. It is doubtful too, that parents would in these days permit two small boys to be alone for many summer days in a park on their own.

Harry's dad referred to Harry's mom as "Toppy." He was sometimes critical of her expressed concern which at times might not seem to have been justified. For example, Harry and I were at the water's edge washing out a utensil when his mom and dad arrived to stay for the weekend. Harry's mom saw us cleaning some fish at the riverside and said, "Harry don't get so close to the river. You might fall in." To that Harry's dad said, "Damn, Toppy. Those kids have been out here for the week all alone and you got here just in time to keep Harry from falling in the river."

Another fishing buddy, Bob Heinemann, was one who accompanied me to Fishpot Creek on a fairly regular basis. We would dig worms in the back of my house, grab our poles and head out. Bob lived at the last house up the street on Boyd Avenue, the house separated from mine by Hildebrand's (next door) and the Aplin house up from mine toward Jefferson.

Bob and Sarah Aplin had a daughter named Gloria, who was into dramatics and who organized neighborhood plays performed in the Aplin garage.

Marty Weisenberg tells the story of when he worked at the Valley Park Elevator (The Mill) on a part time basis in the 40's. Paint was placed in a Gallon glass jar and fixed on the mixer. Metal containers had been forsaken during the war years. The jar shattered and paint went in all directions. Marty found it amusing and could not contain his laughter to see the surroundings being unintentionally decorated, but Louis Pedrotti, who often managed the Elevator, saw nothing

The History Of Valley Park

funny about it. For quite some time, the residue of that "spill" was in evidence in the shelving and on the floor.

A resident in the forties and fifties on Fern Ridge was Kathy Kovac. She used to baby sit Julie (Boyd) Dolan often when her parents and the Boyd families went out. Glenn Boyd and Dee Boyd (brothers) ran an excavation and grading company and Kathy's father, John Kovac, owned County Refrigeration and Heating Co. The Boyd Contracting Company had a contract with the St. Louis Zoo when extensive excavating and site preparation was ongoing in an extensive updating. Kathy recalls the Valley Park Schools multiple purpose building which served as a roller rink, among the more common gymnasium activities. Folks came from around Valley Park to take part in the roller skating. Kathy remembered Judy Priddy as the "champ" among the skaters.

An event that closed out the 40's decade involved a train derailment north of the Marshall crossing on the Frisco and opposite the Missouri Pacific Didian Avenue viaduct. Some associate this incident more directly with the Marshall Avenue crossing. Kathy Kovac recalls that her father took her to the site to observe and allowed her and a sister to pick up one each of the thousands of Hershey bars which had been spilled. Mildred Walker noted that youngsters arrived on the scene and grabbed up candy bars until railroad detectives noticed their activity and demanded that the candies be handed over. The candy bars were placed in an area chosen by the railroad detectives who then moved away from the storage site. With the stash unguarded, Marshal Gus Cox motioned for the youngsters to come over and pick up some candy bars and head straight home. The youngsters happily obliged. So near the end of the year 1949 there was considerable amount of additional chocolate enjoyed in a given time in a number of Valley Park homes.

Leonard Seville recalled that, in addition to the candy bars, there was a large quantity of canned milk in the spillage.

Didian Avenue, a short half-block street, running generally east-west before it turns under the old Missouri Pacific Railroad viaduct, was named after the owner of the property just to the south west and fronting on Forest Avenue and Didian. The large two story home there was purchased by the Catholic Church and became the Sacred Heart High School. It was closed near the mid-forties because of low enrollment and sold to Mary Babke. It later was razed and returned to the ownership of the Church, utilized as a parking lot.

The Lions Club Den was the latter 1940's scene of a dinner-dance given by the employers and the Textile

The History Of Valley Park

Union, the employee organization of the Absorbent Cotton Company. Mr. Gibbons, President of Absorbent Cotton, furnished the orchestra. Several City officials furnished the refreshments.

In the mid forties, a man known to the townspeople as Fireman Jones, had been bringing a food cart to school in the absence of a school cafeteria, later installed in the basement of the high school. This was Charles Jones, who passed away in 1946 and his passing was noted with regrets by students and townspeople.

August 20, 1944, a memorial to WWII was dedicated adjacent the old City Hall on Marshall Avenue. The master of ceremonies was George Bradshaw, Superintendent of Valley Park Schools. Featured speaker was State Senator Richard Ralph, Valley Park resident. He gave a stirring speech in which he talked about what the typical member of service wanted. "Not the glory or honor he deserves," said Ralph, but "All he wants to do is to get the dirty, damned job over with and come home." The Mayor was William J. Brignole, Sr. and his son, William, Jr., did the ceremonial flag raising. "Bill" Brignole, Jr. would later become Fire Chief of the Valley Park Fire District. The memorial was later abandoned and a new one constructed at the site of the new City Hall which occupied the old Benton School.

Through The 20th Century

Railroad traffic ran a close second to the Meramec River in the town's history. In the early forties, two members of the class of '47 (the author and his classmate, Burel Thomas) would hurry through lunch and rush to the Missouri Pacific Railroad mail pitch site and wait for the train. There was a boarded up wall against which a mail bag was thrown out of the train as it roared through. An elevated arm with an attached mail bag to be "hooked" by an arm extended from the train's mail car was the means by which mail left for the St. Louis mail service distribution. It was a cheap thrill to hide behind the boarded wall and watch the action which only lasted for seconds.

In a display of post war patriotism, a high school assembly celebrated Washington's and Lincoln's birthdays simultaneously, getting the jump on the more current practice of combining the two and calling it President's Day. Shirley Rittenhouse acted as chair and introduced Bill Villhard who spoke about Lincoln's social life and Charles Dunn, who talked about Lincoln's political life. Nancy Newman recited the Gettysburg address and Barbara West summarized political life. Mr. Williams, history teacher, reminded students of the great contributions of Washington and his (Washington's) contemporaries.

Near the end of the 45-46 school year when a dance was held in the high school gym, Harold Workman furnished a ride in his Ford for the author and three other high school students-Burel Thomas, Alfred Cooley, and Donald Hart. While the car traveled down Big Bend east of 141 at a high speed, Harold was urged by a couple of the passengers to "Dump it in 80. Dump it 80." The car reached a speed well above that and missed the turn past the Dougherty Ferry (Forest Avenue) intersection. It flip- flopped and then rolled over twice. Disheveled, the five crawled from the wreckage. Luckily only one suffered a break – a collar bone fracture sustained by Alfred Cooley. The day following, the site was viewed by the passengers and it was noted the car had missed a utility pole by only about eighteen inches. Had the car exited Big Bend a little farther to the right, someone else would have had to write this story.

In the Class of '47 Commencement, the President of the Student Council proclaimed that when an atomic bomb fell on a Japanese city, it did more than diminish the effect of geographic boundaries. It also, he said, "…broke the fetters of nationalism which have chained education through the centuries." That was a false prophesy since nationalism at this writing is alive and well in Valley Park as elsewhere in the United States. It remains to be seen how long those chains will bind to a considerable degree.

As Fairy May (Steele) Hollerich recalls, her VPHS Class of '44 was the first graduating class to attend all twelve years in the Valley Park School District. One member of that class was Howard George, who would later become the Mayor of Manchester. A street in Manchester is named after him. While Mayor, he was elected as President of the St. Louis County Municipal League. Members of that class remember Algebra in the mornings at 9:15 being disturbed by a streamliner that came through town and also recall a party at Anne Zeiser's home with the brick patio and built in BBQ pit.

Fairy May gives us a great account of her experiences as a telephone operator in the early days of the telephone company in Valley Park. She served on a part time basis as an operator. Here is her account in her own words:

> When I was sixteen years old, I applied for and got a job with Southwestern Bell Telephone Company as an operator in their Valley Park office. Mrs. Stokes was the manager and an operator, an older woman, Miss Burke, was a full time operator. Often high school students were hired as part-time operators. The first year I worked their, Dorothy Rue and I were the junior operators.
>
> The switchboard was a very old model. It was a magneto style which meant that if the electricity

The History Of Valley Park

went out one could operate the board by turning a crank on the side.

The switchboard was designed with what looked like small, round, black marbles. When someone rang in, the marble would become red. Beneath each "marble" was a "jack" or connector. A "jack" was a hole in the switchboard. On a shelf in front of the operator was a row of twin plugs and a row of switches. When the operator saw a red flash, she would insert an answering plug into the jack and flip a matching switch forward to connect her head set with the caller. In her operator voice whe would say, "Number please." When she was given a number, she would put a calling plug into the called number and flip the matching switch backward to ring the phone of the person called. The operator would stay on the line until someone answered or if there was no answer she would so inform the caller. If someone answered, the operator would flip the switch to the center position which closed the connection to her headset.

There was no signal when the parties were through talking, so the operator at various times would have to go on line and say, "Waiting. Waiting"

Through The 20th Century

If no one answered, the operator would pull both plugs to break the connection.

The operator's interruption was not always welcomed or met with silence. Often the operator would get comments like, "Get off the line, you nosey busybody."

There were a significant number of party lines in Valley Park. A party line involved more than one person on a line (sometimes there were as many as fifteen parties on one line). The operator had to remember the name and the ring for each person on the party line. If someone called 15F4, the operator would have to make one long ring and four short rings

Other people did not call by numbers. They would just say, "Get me the drug store" or "Get me Joe's Tavern". Often children would call and say, "I want Grandma" or "I want Aunt Nell." The operator needed to be familiar with those numbers. To call someone outside of the area, the operator had special trunks to plug into. For long distance, the operator had to write out a slip with the caller's number, the time and the number to be called. The number would then be passed to another operator.

The History Of Valley Park

At the end of the day these tiny slips were sorted and filed.

Looking back, I am awed by the responsibility put upon a sixteen year old. If someone called in and said there was a fire, the operator had to ask for details and then set off the fire alarm. (This would always light up the switchboard and numerous callers would want to know where the fire was). First the operator had to contact the volunteer firemen and give them directions to the fire. Then one by one, she would answer each caller's curiosity about the location.

When there was danger of flooding, the Corp of Engineers called and gave the operator the stages of the river. In turn, calls were answered about the river and in some cases, people who might be in danger were called.

In case of medical emergencies, the operator was supposed to know where to reach the doctor if his office didn't answer.

The night shift, eleven p.m. to seven a. m., was supposed to be a quiet time. But it wasn't always so. Classmates called for assignments and help with homework. Once a woman called at 2:00 a.m.

and asked for help making jelly. Her kerosene stove wasn't working. She never knew she was getting directions from a sixteen year old! Another woman called and wanted to talk about her son who hadn't gotten home that evening. Sometimes people just needed to hear another voice. Often people would call for the time in the early hours of the morning and then explain why they called – getting married that day…big test at school, drank too much coffee, etc. The hours 2 to 6 (a.m.) seemed hardest to stay awake. Another operator, I never knew who, would call and read poetry to me. We would drop off without explanation if a call came during the reading.

Being an operator was not the easiest nor the happiest job.

One got to know a lot about the local people just by plugging in their calls – things you couldn't speak about like cheating spouses, boyfriends and girlfriends, drinking people who told you their problems, people in debt with calls from loan companies, people nice to you to your face who cursed you while you were an operator, and people who were hurting and crying into their telephones.

Being an operator was a people experience!

The History Of Valley Park

The author can vouch for the simplicity of telephone service near its beginnings in Valley Park. In some of my initial uses of the telephone I would ring the operator and she would say, "Number please, Kennard?" I would say "I want to talk to Harry.," and the call was completed.

LONG TERM PERSPECTIVES

NOW AND THEN there is an opportunity to obtain a long term perspective from select individuals who have enjoyed a life that spanned many years. Such is the case with at least two of those associated closely with Valley Park.

Earl Messerla remembers Valley Park when he entered school in 1913, and attended school from about 2 miles south of Valley Park. His family moved to that location when he was two years old after having been born in Valley Park. He and his brother walked to the Hill School on Meramec Station Road. His first teacher was Miss Kaechele, whom he called a "wonderful teacher and a very dear person." He remained a friend of hers through the years until the time of her passing.

Dr. Knabb came to school to vaccinate all of the students. He would take a small glass vial and break the tip off to create a sharp edge. Then a student's arm would be scratched until it bled slightly and the serum would then be applied to the blood. Students would scream and cry even before the doctor gave each scratch in his or her turn.

The History Of Valley Park

Messerla recalled the great flood of 1915, washing away the bridge and prohibiting the walk to Valley Park until a ferry was inaugurated by Valley Park businessmen. This ferry was just west of the railroad bridge crossing and the charges were ten cents for a horse and wagon and five cents for pedestrians, except students who crossed without charge.

At times, in spite of parental admonition against it, he walked across the railroad bridge, and happily, was never on the bridge when a train came through. A big dedication ceremony took place when the new bridge built in 1917 was opened. Hundreds of people gathered around the bridge and after a ceremonial christening with a bottle of champagne broken over the rail by Marilyn Knabb (daughter of Dr. Knabb), there were speeches by Senator Richard Ralph, citizen of Valley Park and prominent attorney. After the festivities at the bridge, the crowd went to Arnold's Grove where free barbeque beef sandwiches and soda were served on tables that were set up for the purpose.

A fond memory was receiving the diploma from the elementary school from his teacher, Mr. Henry Williams. That was May, 1921. Mr Williams subscribed to the addage, "Spare the rod and spoil the child." But he was a wonderful teacher. Hank, as he was called in his absence, was well educated, honest and a real gentleman.

Through The 20th Century

For one who had the greatest impact "on my young life", Messerla said he would have to choose Mr. Williams. He closed his comments with a quote, "A small pebble tossed into a placid pool can cause many ripples."

George James began observations about his life with a memory of Harry Truman.

He remembered when the boss in Kansas City, Tom Pendergast, helped Truman get elected. Truman had a picture of Pendergast on the wall behind his desk and some associates told Truman he should take it down in view of the fact that Pendergast was convicted of serious offenses. James quoted Truman as having said, "No, I won't take it down. He helped me get where I am." "He refused," said James, and "I kinda admired him for that."

"I remember being out in Kansas City, some guys stopped me on the street. They said to come in and vote. I told them I couldn't vote there and they insisted. So I went in to vote and they said, 'you already voted this morning.'"

He was born in 1903. His wife was born in 1905 and lost her father when she was ten years old. Her father was thirty-five years old when he died.

"My dad had that store over there on St. Louis Avenue. (It was James Mercantile). People came out here for the

The History Of Valley Park

weekend and later on some built club houses here and stayed in them over the weekend."

"I remember a guitar player who used to sit on the sidewalk over there and play. We kids used to gather round and listen to him play the guitar and sing."

"We used to roller skate and ice skate. I remember a bunch going out on and up the Meramec to the bridge. (a distance of about four blocks). It was frozen over… so I saw the other kids going out there and I did too. I skated all the way to the Meramec bridge and the ice was going like this… (James moved his hand up and down.) That was scary. I wasn't scared so much at the time but later on, it scared me after I thought about it." He remembered doing a lot of roller skating on the side walks.

"When I was five or six, I came downstairs with a sandwich in one hand and a pickle in the other. Boys were outside playing ball. I wanted to go out and play with them. We had a rain barrel to catch water from the roof run off and I stopped and looked down inside it and leaned over too far." He fell in head first and a man saw his plight and pulled him out. James noted "…it wasn't funny then but looking back… it was funny. "His favorite past time now? "Enjoying my kids." He and his wife were the parents of Evelyn, Patsy,

Through The 20th Century

Barbara, and Ken. Ken mowed the lawn during the time we were visiting with his dad.

He remembers the 1915 flood when the water came up above the top of the door on the first floor. (This was in the family James Mercantile store) His brother would dive under the door top and come up on the other side and retrieve canned goods to be taken upstairs. A second story porch was used by some as a diving platform while the river was up high.

He worked at the Copper Clad Range Company in St Louis as one of his earliest jobs. "I guess the first real job was with Scullin Steel. I worked there forty six years and retired. At that time (when working) you could get back and forth because trains were running in and out of the City. I bought round trip tickets…twelve cents each way and the conductor would punch the ticket when you used the first part." In another time later, he remembered, he walked from the street car line in Kirkwood to his home. During one such walk, a lady pulled her car over and gave him a ride. She said she noticed he had a lunch pail and knew he was on his way home from work.

He had a motorcycle for about eight years and remembers riding up "mile hill" (the upgrade on Marshall Road toward Kirkwood) when it was a dirt road. "I sold the bike to a guy at Scullin Steel. He let a friend borrow it and the friend tipped it over and put a hole in the gas tank." When it was returned to the owner, the borrower had stuck a piece of gum in the hole. The owner discovered a serious leakage when he began riding it. James laughed at the situation as he recalled it.

James recalled Scullin management bringing truckloads of black people from the south when the Scullin workers went on strike.

At Scullin, James received pay in gold coins and it was not until being employed there for a time that the payments came in the form of cash in an envelope and in the late twenties, checks were being issued.

Asked about prohibition, James said, "I think that was the worst thing they ever did… It just made the gangsters make a lot of money. There was a man down at work who loaded his car with beer and took it over to Illinois and sold it. They never bothered him about it."

In 1926 "I was remodeling my house. I bought this house for twelve hundred dollars at a sheriff's sale over in Clayton." George Booth, a good friend, said he would see to it that a mortgage for the remodeling would be available. The payments were twenty eight dollars per month until things got tough. He would report to Scullin for work and he and others would be told they couldn't go back to work for about three weeks. The plant would close two and three weeks at a time. He went to the bank on Third and St. Louis and told Harry Vance that he needed to get a longer term loan because he didn't think he could keep making the payments. At the time James was making about fifteen dollars a week. "Harry told me, 'You go on home, George. Just pay the interest only on your loan and begin making regular payments when you can.'" James said, "They don't do that any more" and he smiled.

James identified a milk man, Allen Hawkins, and he told the milk man one day that he would have to quit delivering milk because "I can't pay you for it." James said the milk man told him, "George, your kids need this milk. I am going to keep on delivering it and you can catch up paying me when your work gets better." James said, "They don't do that any more either."

"In WWII, brother Tom was rejected here (flat feet or something), but he went to Canada and joined there. The other two brothers joined here."

James recalled the time his brother Dick (when he was City Marshal) was instructed by the Mayor to ticket every car that doesn't have a city sticker. The first cars ticketed were those of two of the Mayor's friends, and there was immediately less pressure to do the ticketing. Marshal Dick James would issue warnings and allow two or three weeks for motorists to get stickers. "There were hard times," James said, "and my brother knew that." He (the brother) would sometimes find out about a serious financial problem a family had and he would order a ton of coal and have it delivered without identifying himself as the benefactor.

"State Senator Richard Ralph was a neighbor and a regular guy. He and his friends played croquet in the yard where the sod was stripped and made smooth with sand for a court." James said there was a joke about Sen. Ralph kicking his ball a little closer to the wicket when no one was looking.

The first U. S. President James recalled after his Harry Truman comment, was Woodrow Wilson. Wilson said he would keep us out of war and then we had war declared. 'My dad was a Republican but voted for Wilson because of the promise to keep us out of war. He (my dad) …had that against Wilson. Calvin Coolidge was a good president. He came before Hoover. Hoover got a lot of criticism but I thought he was pretty good."

"Franklin D. Roosevelt? Well I guess the best thing he ever did was bring in that Social Security. I think he was well liked. I think he was a good president. They didn't tell him what to do. I think he told them what to do."

"Well, Truman. I already talked about him. He wouldn't take that picture down. That was something I liked about him. Eisenhower was a better general than he was president."

On John Kennedy. "I didn't vote for him" but James thought "…he could have been a good president but didn't get much chance. I think that (the assassination) was a put up job. I think Johnson was a good president.

Nixon could have been all right if he hadn't permitted that break-in. He looked better some time later. Carter was a better farmer than president."

"Reagan was lucky in picking good people around him. The spending was too high."

George Bush? "Well, I voted for him. Maybe because I am a Republican. I think he was fair and a pretty good president."

"Bill Clinton would have been a good president except for all his doings. He was very smart and did a lot of good things."

How about the greatest change during his lifetime?

The History Of Valley Park

"Air travel," he said. He didn't do much of it. He flew to Arizona and back and each time was glad to get on the ground. On the return, the pilot announced that passengers could look down and see Joplin and Springfield. He said, "I looked up."

Asked to what he attributes his long life he said it was mostly "good cooking and keeping busy." And asked if he could make one wish and knew it come true he said, "Peace. I don't understand why people can't get along. People ought to let other people have their views and do their own thing and just get along with each other."

Some reflections are furnished by Glenn E. Moon, who came to the Valley Park area in 1941 and lived in a club house on the south side of the Meramec.

His stepfather, Henry Friend arrived to work on the Tyson Valley Powder Dump and at the Weldon Springs Plant. Glenn would later move to Sixth Street and Benton in Valley Park. Glenn recalled a project which he and Marty Weisenburg teamed up to complete while in Valley Park High School. It was a rocket and the design came from a Popular Mechanics magazine. When the time came for the launch, the rocket soared to a height of about four to six feet before it gave up.

Through The 20th Century

Joseph Stephan and Wilfred "Red" Henderson were City Clerks prior to the time that Moon was elected to that office. Moon served as City Clerk for 34 years and was Water Commissioner also. He recalled the 1982 flood when the water works building had the only phone the City had in operation. It was located on the south side of Marshall where the Meramec Valley Bank was located after that water plant was abandoned. Surrounding phones were out of service also. Nat Dubman made use of the phone in the water works building to conduct some of his business at Carol House Furniture across the street.

Caroline Bibbs is remembered as the first Afro-American to be elected to the Board of Education. She was an activist in local politics and Republican Party politics and was selected by Nixon to make a friendship visit to Africa. Her church on Marshall Road had a Gospel sing each year with guests from near and far.

When the Valley Park water system came into being shortly after incorporation, Oscar Hildebrandt began as operator and served in that capacity until his death. He was an eccentric and viewed the water works as a personal possession. Glenn Moon tells the story of being water commissioner and the necessity of digging up a valve near the plant, when Oscar made a threat with a hammer for "messing with his water." Oscar could be seen trudging

The History Of Valley Park

up Meramec Station Road at the end of the work day. He had a gauge in his basement at home which enabled him to read the water level in storage tanks and he enjoyed reading Popular Mechanics.

Some of the people who Moon remembers best were Sarah Aplin, Mayor Ben Beckett, George James, Sherman "Pee Wee" Maine, Jess Stewart, Police Chiefs Louis Brown and Gus Cox, Harper Rue, Joe Hertwerk, Joe Stephan and "Red" Henderson. The person elected as Marshal served as Chief of Police. Reno Weggemann, Gus Cox, and Louis Brown served in that capacity.

Sherman "Pee Wee" Maine, had long time service on the volunteer fire department until it was formally established as the Valley Park Fire Protection District. While he served in that capacity, there was seldom a fire at which he did not take part in efforts to extinguish a blaze and save property.

Chief Louis Brown, after his retirement, was the victim of a gas leak which invaded the sun room of his home. He was getting ready to exit the sun room to light a grill on his patio and switched on his lighter, resulting in a gas explosion which burned him severely and brought about his death a short time later.

George Metal had been a home builder in the Bevo Mill area of St. Louis and would become Building Commissioner in Valley Park for many years. He is remembered also for the great tomatoes grown in his garden. His daughter, Virginia "Ginny"Hiscox, was a secretary for the City for a considerable time and served well in that capacity.

Dorothy (Chuchetti) Kettler was born in 1925 and her earliest recollection of life in Valley Park was her dad's grocery store and her older brother Joe who was already 15 years old when she was born. Another brother Frank was 16 years old.

That store opened in 1929 and the daily delivery of groceries, riding with Joe, resulted in customers always inviting them to have something to eat. All the people were so friendly. She still remembers the store's phone number. It was #13 and her home phone was #100. Visitors, like Don Waters and Ralph Thomas came into the store and sat on the top of the freezer shelf, listening to the radio blaring music.

At a later date, age 12, she would plead for the opportunity to drive by sitting in the driver's seat as her brother came to the car. There were times when she succeeded and then there the times when her brother was less likely to give in to the idea. She recalls her brother telling her to get over… because he is in a hurry to get things done… had a hot date in Catawissa. "He had many girl friends," She said. Dorothy wondered where Catawissa was and inquired until she learned it's location. That location was confirmed when she worked at the West County Landfill and saw a truck with a Catawissa address painted on the door. As to the under aged driving, it was not at all unusual in certain circumstances. Dorothy recalled seeing Harry Lee Simpson's sons driving trucks all over the property where the sand and gravel operation was located. "They were good drivers," she said.

A special thrill came when she was permitted to ride with her brother when he became fire chief and the thrill was enhanced when he turned on the siren and had the light flashing as they went to the location of a fire in the chief's car.

Dorothy attended Sacred Heart School from elementary through high school and was one of only three – Betty Hagen, Betty Riefling, and her – in their graduating class there. The high school was located just to the southeast of Didian between Ann Avenue and Forest Avenue. That building was later occupied by the Babka family. Dorothy recalled that Libby, Pat, and Jean Burdette lived there for a time after the Babka's and talked of the house being haunted. A woman in the Didian family was said to have committed suicide there. Stories were told of a rocking chair rocking with no one in it and other unexplainable occurrences.

Shortly after her marriage to Bud Kettler, they moved into a house on Ann Avenue. A favorite person was Lorraine Smith who had retired from teaching at Lindberg High School. "She was fun to be with," Dorothy said, and friendships with other older people developed – with Ann Humphries, Vi Stubblefield, and Ethel Scholl.

Dorothy's mother was a Lady Lion and she and her Lady Lion friends held monthly luncheons at different homes in the community. Her mother often gave a sandwich to a man down on his luck during the depression when that man came to the back door of the house. These men often came to the back door of houses to ask for a bite to eat and were usually successful in obtaining a hand-out.

The most memorable event for Bill Hansel was the year the Valley Park High baseball team won the state tournament in 1988. So many of the townspeople as well as the student body turned out to support the players and baseball Coach Gregston.

Harvey Moore attended boot camp and served in the same company as Bill during the Korean conflict. They remained friends in Korea and after the conflict. Bill was married to Miriam Lochman by her father, the Pastor of the Lutheran Church, who gave Bill continuous support and is one of those best remembered by Bill. The floods endured by

The History Of Valley Park

Valley Park and the manner in which people came together to sand bag or assist families in moving to safety has left an impression on Bill as evidence of a genuine community spirit which involved helping those in need. Coach Tschanon, (Bill isn't sure about the spelling) was one of the faculty at VPHS remembered best along with Mrs. Lattimore. With evidence of ability in basketball, a coach from Mehlville tried to recruit Bill to attend school in Mehlville. Bill thinks the changes in the buildings of Valley Park Schools deserve an important place in the community's history.

Calvin (Cal) Hedrick was born in Bixby, Missouri, and came to Valley Park in the mid sixties after the building in St. Louis in which he lived was sold and necessitated a move. It was to the Valley Park area and very soon into Valley Park proper. During WWII he worked at Wagner Electric and operated a grinder which was part of the process of making radios for the Boeing B-29. His work was deemed critical for the war effort and he was deferred a number of times from the draft. Cal and his wife Dorothy established and operated a dry cleaning establishment for 31 years along Highway 141 just south of Vance Road. He was a member of the Lions Club and is especially proud of the help the Lions organization has given to those with eyesight problems and diabetes over the years. His membership in the Lions dates from 1957 and his membership in the Masons was almost as long. He noted the spirit of cooperation among Valley Park residents in helping each other during floods and other difficult situations. "Everyone pitched in," he said. "There was no hesitance when it came to helping."

In 1978 Cal was elected Mayor and served until 1982, the year in which Valley Park experienced another severe flood.

In 1982 Fred Palmer was elected Mayor and a short time after he was sworn in, the severe flood of that year occurred.

His administration promoted the levee project, scheduled for completion in 2005. His trips to Washington, D. C. to testify before congressional committees and the assistance of Col. Lee McKinney along with write-in campaigns to encourage congressional funding put the levee project on track. During his administration, four successful annexations took place, some to the north and some to the west, and a revised housing code was placed in effect. His office communicated with the citizenry through a "Mayor's Newsletter" in the hopes of keeping that citizenry better informed. Beautification of the railroad right of way received important attention and he pushed for installation of sidewalks along old Meramec Station Road.

The History Of Valley Park

Some of the events in Wanda (Messerla) Lister's life have been mentioned earlier but a few other observations by her are in order. She remembers best her neighbors, the Hendersons and Dr. Frank P. Knabb. The Hendersons – Betty, Doris, Bob and Don played games together with her. The Henderson's parents, "… were like second parents to me." Dr. Knabb, the family physician for 20 years faithfully attended Wanda's younger sister who died at the age of four with scarlet fever. Dr. Knabb spent much time at the Messerla home until the sister was hospitalized. That sister was buried on Christmas Day in 1932. Even though Dr. Knabb was much older, he practiced part time and when Wanda and Dave were getting married in 1946, Dr. Knabb had performed their blood work in his own home even though his mobility was poor. Wanda and her husband moved to Florida and looked forward to their 55th wedding anniversary to be reached in 2001.

Harry Simpson was born in Valley Park and became one of its prominent businessmen. The Simpsons had the first gravel plant in St. Louis County and in later years Harry Simpson marketed Quickcrete which became a staple in many of the hardware and builder supply stores locally and in widespread locations.

The land adjacent the sand and gravel operation along Marshall in the east end of the City was a part of the City's

Through The 20th Century

first annexation and the sand and gravel pit became a lake which furnished a site for fishermen. The plant was abandoned when Simpson and Wayne Kennedy, the then Parks and Recreation Director for St. Louis County, made a deal whereby Simpson would donate one-half of the property and the County would purchase the other half with a grant from the federal level. It became Simpson County Park and is one of the more attractive parks in the County with the lake formed by the one-time dredging operation of Simpson's operation on the north side of Marshall.

The plant for processing sand products was established on the south side of Marshall Road in close proximity to where the plate glass factory had been. Simpson bought many metal parts, then designed and built a hiker which was used in the operation. By designing it and building it himself he saved many thousands of dollars. He often designed and built many of the major rigs used by his company. He joked about one of the locals stealing gas from the Simpson gravel plant hoist in earlier days.

He recalls the temperature being below zero for 15 days around 1932 or 1933. Frank Harles worked in his dad's garage. That was Simpson's Garage, built by Ray Woods, on the west side of Highway 141 at Marshall Road. We have noted already Simpson's admiration for Henry Williams, Simpson's teacher in Valley Park High with Simpson's class being the first graduating class in 1936. He remembers a retirement party for Mr. Williams and recalls his last seeing him at the Central Hardware store in Kirkwood.

Harry Simpson could name the sources for the purchase of the legally forbidden beverages in Valley Park during prohibition and also remembers being challenged by Francis Dean, or dared, to grab a live wire while attending a party at Harry Barber's house. He recalled a Jennie pilot who was killed at Lake Hill when his craft hit a guy wire. He was with Glenn "Speedy" Neel when they went to the State prison for a baseball game against the prisoners. "Speedy" Neel was the son of Vincent Neel, who was President of the School Board at the time. Harry remembers barber Lortz and John Goree, the Union Electric employee mentioned earlier. Simpson recalled that Jimmie Huskisson was an engineer on the Frisco prior to his purchase and operation of Hotel Hodnett. In Harry's opinion, the organization which probably made the greatest contribution to the community over the years was the Lions Club.

Through The 20th Century

A SUCCESS STORY

In 1952, a young man, 23 years old, was going door to door in Valley Park selling wares out of the back of a van.

He was born in Poland, moved to Canada with his parents at the age of 10 and to De Soto, Missouri, with his parents while in his teens, and then to the St. Louis area. Enjoying some success with his door to door salesmanship, Nat Dubman purchased his van and began selling wares, primarily clothing, out of the back of that van. It was not an uncommon sight to see housewives looking over garments which were carried on racks in the back of the van. Nor was it uncommon to see a housewife carrying a purchased article of clothing into her house.

Dubman began selling in communities near Valley Park and would soon be in a business where customers came to him. In 1964, he purchased and renovated an old store west of Highway 141 and opened Carol House Furniture. A few years later the store was moved to the site of the old lumber yard on the north side of Marshall Avenue west of Meramec Valley Bank. There was an extensive remodeling and enlargement of that structure and customers were drawn from a wide area.

Mr. Dubman talked about his parents with an obvious feeling of admiration, noting that he took advice from his father in the matter of making life's decisions. "Parents are smart," he said. "They know a lot and it's important to listen to them. "Business grew steadily and in 1983 Dubman opened another store at Page and Lindberg in north St. Louis County. In a brief visit there with Mr. Dubman the author suggested that "This is a long way from selling out of the back of a van." He responded saying, "When I look around here, I can hardly believe it." He observed that one of the greatest thrills a man could have was to have his children working with him as partners in a business and know that they would take it over at a later time. He has certainly enjoyed that kind of thrill. His son, Brooke, and daughter, Amy, were partners in the business and have taken over the management.

For Nat Dubman, Valley Park was certainly a "City of Opportunity," but he understood well the admonition that the trouble with opportunity is that it always comes disguised as hard work.

Nathan "Nat" Dubman died May 16, 2001, following a heart attack at Forest Park Hospital at the age of 72. He was a past board member of the Jewish Federation of St. Louis and the Jewish Community Center. The Valley Park Carol House furniture store would still stand at the end of the 20th Century a short block east of Highway 141 on Marshall Avenue just east of the old Frisco Railroad tracks.

In the 60's, the City's attention was focused on the problem of untreated sewage and the lack of sewer lines in the west/northwestern part of the City. Ben Beckett (elected in the 50's) served as Mayor throughout the 60's and into the 70's. His administration was one marked with frugality When a proposal came forward his first question was "Now where are we going to get the money for this."

He championed the push for sewers and treatment of sewage. The early 60's saw the establishment of a three cell lagoon for primary, secondary and tertiary treatment. The City maintained the lagoons and in the later 60's, a bond issue was passed which extended sewer lines and continued the treatment in the lagoon system, until the Metropolitan Sewer District installed a treatment facility to deal with sewage from Valley Park and the watershed beyond. Mayor Beckett was always amiable but persistent in refusing to support any project unless he knew "Where's the money coming from" to fund it. He was capable of laughing at barbs sometimes aimed at him although these were few and mostly in good fun. On one occasion, when Ben, the City

The History Of Valley Park

Clerk Moon, Chief Brown and a couple of the Aldermen were attending a baseball game, the loaded car approached a police officer whom Chief Brown knew and asked about some favored treatment for a parking place. One of the car's occupants said, "We have our Chief of Police here and the Mayor and we would like to be able to park close by the stadium." The officer, who was known to many as Casey, said, "The hell with the Mayor but if you have the Police Chief with you, park right up against the stadium there" as he pointed out a spot. "I'll look after your car." Mayor Becket had a good laugh at Casey's comment.

Mayor Beckett encouraged the City's participation in the Municipal League and the City was always represented at League meetings at the County and State levels. It was during his term that a problem with Laclede Gas came to the forefront. Many residents wanted gas service but Laclede would not provide it unless it involved a good number of users in a confined locale. Petitions were circulated in a number of areas and Laclede eventually provided gas service to just about all who asked for it.

Mayor Beckett brought a history of his own to the community and shared it with others. For example, he told of a situation earlier in his life when he saw an appendix removed from a man with a kitchen knife being the operating tool while the man was lying on the kitchen table.

He served until 1972 and then filed for election to the Mayor's office again in 1976, winning by a considerable margin. He died near the end of 1976 and the author was elected to fill the unexpired term. which ended in 1978. Mayor Beckett is remembered by having Beckett Memorial Drive (formerly First Street), which runs parallel to the old Frisco Railroad, named in his honor.

The History Of Valley Park

STUDENT HISTORIANS

Helen Jones Gansler, a teacher in Valley Park Schools, supervised a project called Span Reading Program (formerly talented reading).

It included a history of Valley Park written by Connie Jones in 1936 and already referenced. Students conducted interviews with citizens in Valley Park and told their stories in a publication called "*Reflections of a Proud Community*," printed in the mid 1980's. Students who participated in the interviews or assisted otherwise and whose names appear in the project publication were Tim Siebe, Matthew Peek, Scott James, Kerrie Barton, Shirine Doud, Toni Phillips, Lisa Wall, and Latonya Blevins, Michelle Brown, Cammie Robinson, Chris Harwell. Antonio Philllip. Elaina Johnson, Lisa Singer, Bryan Wilson, Debbie Duff, Steve Dyche, Wendy Hopper, Jennifer Fingers, Amy Wood, Tawanda Malone and David Aubuchon…

Others who made contributions interviewing or otherwise were: Deann Bantel, John Nickel, Felicia Norwood, Chantelle Ishmon, and Darnetta Sloan.

Through The 20th Century

Many of the accounts in the *Reflections of a Proud Community* are similar to and in some cases identical to the authors accounts, since the author had the opportunity to know almost all of the citizens interviewed and the stories of their times in Valley Park. Some accounts came from the recorded student interviews.

One of the citizens interviewed by the students was Rachel Wideman, mentioned here for the first time. She was born in 1913 and came to Valley Park at the age of seven. She remembers that most of the streets were of cinders and if you fell, you ended up "with a knee full of cinders."

There were not many beauty shops back then and sometimes girls used steel curlers which hurt a lot when you slept on them but girls "…did sacrifice comfort for pretty curls." Rachel Wideman confirmed the view of Ruth Van Dover that not many people went to the doctor but did have a lot of home remedies.

Rachel married young, at sixteen. It wasn't unusual in those days. Robert Melvin Wideman, known as Melvin, was a hard worker who, after various jobs including one with Mississippi Steel, started Wideman Trucking which was a prominent company for many years in Valley Park.

Rachel and Melvin had three children: Fayetta, Lorraine, and Michael. Lorraine's daughter, Lisa Gross, became

The History Of Valley Park

a teacher and took part in some of the compilation of *Reflections of a Proud Community*.

The author remembers Rick Gross, Lisa's brother, whose father Fred assisted with my Khoury League Baseball team on which Rick played. Speaking of baseball, Jess Hill, mentioned as a manager of one of the first boys baseball teams, also managed a young men's team. It was he who paid Loren Hewitt fifteen cents to retrieve foul balls during games. Loren was a member of the first class to publish Val-E-Views (the yearbook) under the supervision of Anne Zeiser Ritter.

The old hotel, described herein earlier, was the birthplace of Harvey Moore. After the decline in tourist patronage, some rooms were rented out to residents.

He remembers the spelling contests, usually pitting the boys against the girls, and "you had to sit down when you misspelled a word."

Since automobiles were few, kids could sleigh ride on Meramec Station Road. Recreation usually centered around the home. It was fun listening to the radio, imagining the "view" of what we were hearing.

Harvey notes that "the only time you went to a hospital was to die. Some died at home too." We never heard about drugs like marijuana or cocaine. Out houses were the most common toilet facilities and for Halloween pranks, these were sometimes tipped over.

Few people had telephones and Harvey observed, "How nice for parents of teenagers today." Harvey was mentioned earlier for sharing a military experience with Bill Hansel, not only in basic training but serving in the same unit during the Korean military action. Harvey was fond of the trips to Forest Park Highlands for the School picnic.

We have quoted him before in connection with the time after the glass company's shut-down, but William Rue was one of those who responded to inquiries for *Reflections of a Proud Community*.

He recalled that Valley Park was a small country town during his boyhood. The fire engine was a small 1930 or 1932 Chevrolet pumper. Later, a 1941 Chevrolet was obtained. A fire resulted in a whistle being blown and many folks would try to go the fire. (See Fairy May (Steel) Hollerrich's account of phone service). The police/fire department and City Hall were all in the same small building on Marshall Avenue. "The police department was an elected one man Marshal with one plain unmarked car."

The City street department consisted of a small dump truck and a pull type grader.

The History Of Valley Park

That whistle also blew at noon each day. There was no mail delivery and people went to the U. S. Post office on Marshall Avenue to pick up their mail. There were two railroad depots in town and trains would stop and drop off passengers and freight. Mail was sometimes tossed out in canvas bags as a train speeded through. There was also a mounted arm device on which the station master could attach a mail bag to be snatched by an arm extended from the train's mail car. One of the highlights of our youth was to watch the trains speed through town. William remembered watching trains going through town loaded with tanks, trucks, jeeps, artillery and train cars filled with military men. Many Frisco trains would stop to take on water from a wooden water tower on the southeast corner of the Frisco Marshall Avenue intersection.

William graduated from VPHS in 1945 and went into the Marine Corps. He noted that most able bodied men in Valley Park joined the service or were drafted when they became eighteen. His graduating class, as he remembers, had five males and fourteen females.

The Tyreys (Owen and Virgie) recalled rationing during World War II. Gasoline and much of the food was rationed. They usually walked everywhere they went as pointed out herein, discussing education.

Through The 20th Century

There was no television in the early forties but programs on the radio furnished good listening and on Sundays it was customary to walk to the Park Theatre to see a show there. Sodas and ice cream were available at the drug store.

After dinner time, the neighborhood kids would get together "…in someone's back yard and play hide and seek or kick the can." Swimming in the summer "in the creek close to our house" (Fishpot Creek) or in the Meramec River were favorites. Lifestyles had a much slower pace, there were no computers or television. Girls played with dolls and boys played with their toy cars and guns. (Owen grew up in a house just north of the one in which Virgie spent her youth and at this writing the Tyreys live in a house built on the corner property where Virgie's house was located during her early years.)

In Betty Finder's response for the *Reflections of a Proud Community,* she noted that Leonard Park was just a weed patch in 1937. There were three swimming pools and a fish fry site with outdoor tables that were nice to go to in the summer.

She remembers the annual Valley Park School picnic at the highlands (Forest Park Highlands) and how the train picked up everyone to "take us to the highlands and bring us home in the evening." The highlands had all kinds of great

The History Of Valley Park

rides, a place to dance, a lot of food stands, and plenty of tables for those who brought picnic baskets. Even so, she thought the most fun of all was "riding that train to and from the highlands." She observed that "People did a lot more walking back then…" because there was not two or three cars in each family. Buses took people to Kirkwood or Maplewood where most shopping was done. The shopping malls that we have today did not exist.

Starting school in 1929, Luella (Wissman) Brockman lived on a farm along Hanna Road and as a small child her dad drove her to school each day in his 1925 Model T Ford. In about the third grade, she bagan walking to school unless it was raining or snowing. There was no such thing as "snow days" back then.

The schools have grown considerably. She noted that in 1932 there was just the high school building housing grades one to twelve. (One through six on the first floor.)

A lot of trains came through town and engines could be heard chugging up the incline toward Kirkwood and we could hear the whistles as the trains came through town. During the war years, troops would wave from the open train windows. There was no air conditioning in the trains then.

Louella's husband, Ray, moved to Valley Park from Webster Groves when he was thirteen years old in 1932.

Ray and his brothers went swimming and boating a lot in the Meramec in days before it became polluted.

(The young historians noted that Mrs. Brockman was renowned for her expertise providing permanents and hair cuts when beauty shops were likely to be found in homes).

A heart wrenching story about Gretchen Brockman, the grand daughter of Ray and Louella Brockman, came about in the mid eighties when Gretchen wrote an account of her bout with cancer and shared it with her classes. She was unable to finish the story and her mother Susan finished it. Susan and Gary Brockman lost their daughter.

One of Gretchen's classmates, Carrie Wideman, wrote a touching post-humus letter to Gretchen, ending with "You will always be alive in my memory forever."

We noted earlier that Dorothy (Cuchetti) Kettler made friends with some who were considerably older than she.

One of those was Ann Humphries. Born in Oxford, Mississippi, on December 3, 1898, in a one room log cabin with a wood burning stove, she came to Valley Park by train at the age of six. Her father was here to run a farm and the family lived in Fenton while their house was being built in Valley Park. She finished schooling after the eighth grade

The History Of Valley Park

and began working at age fourteen. Her work in the Cotton Factory paid forty cents an hour and some girls worked under her supervision for twelve cents an hour.

Mrs. Humphries shared her experience with the young "historians" including the practice of always wearing a dress to school, attending the movies when the cost was five cents, and a gallon of gas was twelve cents. She told how Easter eggs would be dyed with coffee grounds and onion skins. At Christmas time a cedar tree would be decorated with homemade ornaments and pop corn. Real candles would be attached but rarely lighted because of the danger of fire. Soap made from greenwood ash with lye and grease was used for laundry. A wash board was the standard device for clothes washing. Mrs. Humphries was widowed in 1975 with the death of her husband whom she had married in 1913.

As part of the *Reflections of a Proud Community* publication project, grandparents were invited to classes to share their memories. One such visit was by Mr. and Mrs. Loyal Gibbs.

John Cusack, grandson of Mr. and Mrs. Loyal Gibbs brought them to class to share memories. Loyal Gibbs moved to Valley Park in 1934. His wife, Lucille, came from a Czechoslovakian neighborhood in south St. Louis. The Gibbs family occupied a house on Vest Avenue and had four school teachers as boarders. They hired Carrie Turner whose father came to the area to work on the Van Dover estate. It was Carrie who told them about the popular hotel where she remembered afternoon teas and ladies entertaining on the big porches on Benton Street. That street was at the time, one of the most fashionable areas.

In the thirties, eleven trains a day stopped in Valley Park. Weekends were exciting as the pleasure seekers from St. Louis came to fish and canoe the beautiful Meramec River. Frivolity prevailed at the popular dance hall in Arnold's Grove, where even Charles Lindberg came to watch and sometime dance. According to a former citizen, he was shy but had a warm smile.

The heavy 1945 flood made it necessary for the Gibbs family to go by canoe to the Frisco Depot. This was, of course, prior to their move to Ann Avenue. The water was swift and dangerous, they recalled.

People really did have "ice boxes" and the Gibbs couple recalled the practice of people putting up cards in the window with the 25, 50, 75, or 100 upright at the top so the ice man would know how much to deliver.

Grandson John is a graduate of Valley Park High and his grandparents moved to a house off Crescent Avenue. John's parents are Dave and Joan Cusack.

The History Of Valley Park

We heard from Lol Halker earlier but she contributed information to the *Reflections of a Proud Community* project and that contribution tells us that when she arrived in Valley Park with her three sisters and two brothers that there was no bus service. There was, however, trains which ran through town and furnished transportation. Lol attended Sacred Heart School through the eighth grade. For most, this was the end of formal schooling and was a great event. Summertime recreation involved a swim in the Meramec or to Lake Hill Amusement Park where there was an admission charge of twenty five cents. Movies cost ten cents. "As ridiculous as it may sound," she said, "one dollar was a lot of money then."

Winter time recreation could be found by skating on one of the lakes in Lake Hill Amusement Park. It was later drained and became a speedway for auto racing. Kenny and Rusty Wallace got their initial race car experiences at Lake Hill Speedway. Sledding on Meramec Station hill was another winter recreation. It was blocked off from Fern Ridge down to Forest Avenue. Participants were the very young to adults. A big bonfire was kept alive at the top of the hill and down at the end of the slide.

The annual school picnic was a big event and the occasional circus that came to town furnished excitement.

Through The 20th Century

As her contribution to the *Reflections of a Proud Community* publication, Dottie Kassler recalled going to the show every Sunday around 2:00 p.m. where she sat next to her great-grandmother.

Her cousin would accompany her to the show and sometimes ride his bike. In a couple of instances they would ride the bike from the top of Meramec Station Road to Forest Avenue without touching the pedals. "If my parents only knew… " she mused. "You have to understand that there was hardly any automobile traffic in those days."

She often walked to school with Inez Chapman and remembers her sister Joan (Dottie's sister), Barb Shelton and her fixing their hair in banana curls.

Her mom used to wrap ribbons around glasses and then iron them so we could wear them in our hair.

The whole school was housed in one building with grades one to six on the first floor and seven to eight on the second floor. She concluded, "Our lives were a lot simpler then but very happy."

There were five girls in the Jones family and two of them remained in Valley Park and became teachers here – Helen Gansler and Doris Waplehorst.

The History Of Valley Park

Elaine was in Denver, while Marian and Monica were in Phoenix. Helen Gansler observed that people are much more prosperous these days (mid eighties) than was the case in forties and fifties. Back then people kept their cars for many years. You could tell who was attending church by the cars parked in the church lot.

Walking was not only for exercise but a necessary mode of transportation. Taxi service was available along Marshall and Highway 141. A ride to anywhere in town with no charge for extra passengers was fifty cents.

In school the Sisters of Notre Dame always planned activities such as kiddie carnivals, plays, field trips, and guest speakers.

The town was rural and there were plenty of places to pick berries. At age twelve, Helen made as many as four blackberry pies a day. Canning was a common practice as was gardening, raising chickens and making clothes from gunny sacks. A store bought dress was a luxury.

Since the third grade, her teacher, Mrs. Hawkins, was the influence In Lisa Gross's decision to become a teacher. That was when Lisa was eight years old. Lisa gave an overview of grade levels and things remembered. Fourth grade-we learned each state and had "cookouts" focusing on the specialty food of each state. "I gained about five pounds that year." Fifth grade – There were some changeovers in teachers but one that lasted, Miss Bright, in 1986 was one of Lisa's colleagues. In the middle school, desegregation had not yet begun. There were forty five students in the class that moved on to high school. In the year of the *Reflections* publication, there were sixty.

There was no girls basketball team so Lisa and Mary Redmon tried out for the Boys team. She played softball and volleyball under Coach Dauster.

Movies and roller skating in her younger years were replaced by movies and bowling and as main recreations. Summer provided Khoury League softball/baseball and fishing in the Meramec. She and her grandfather used to run a trout line across the Meramec in summer months.

In response to a question from Mary Garza, Lisa noted that she sometimes wore jeans but only the fashionable bell bottoms – (no poodle skirts) or a ribbon in her hair and the students were not permitted to wear shorts to school.

In 1972, the desegregation of St. Louis area schools began and Valley Park was a County school taking part in the program.

In 1993, Free Smith graduated from Valley Park High School after having attended Valley Park Schools since the fourth grade as one of the desegregation students from St. Louis. Free says, "I was one of the first to participate in the desegregation program. I was the second Afro-American on the cheerleading squad, brought back the 'spirit stick' from the Universal Cheerleaders Association camp and earned the privilege to participate in the Christmas parade in England for Queen Elizabeth.

Free will not presume to speak for other deseg students, but says the experience in Valley Park changed her life drastically, instilling a sense of pride and appreciation for opportunity. She was impressed by being allowed to share her own history with other students. Dr. Lea (then Superintendent of Valley Park Schools) gave her the use of the public address system during Black History Month. She gave a short bio of Afro Americans who made a difference with their influence in the world. She expressed gratitude to Dr. Lea, Mrs. Vlahiotis, Mrs. Weidenbenner, and "Senora" Take. Free went to Florissant Community College and then to Webster University and thinks of Valley Park as home.

Coach Frank Wilhite, retired at this writing,, remembers another desegregation student, Ali Jones, who played on the high school varsity basketball team. While in grade school, he had told Coach Wilhite that he was going to be a rapper. "I didn't even know what a rapper was," Wilhite said. According to Free Smith, Ali knew what it was since he became part of the St. Lunatics rap group of which Nelly is a member and was put in charge of Nelly's record label.

After my election as Mayor in 1972, I was fortunate enough to be elected to the Executive Committee of the St. Louis County Municipal League.

There was concern about the antiquated bridge over the Meramec along Highway 141. I sent a letter to the Highway Department asking for a copy of the inspection report on the bridge. I received a letter saying that the bridge was found to be in satisfactory condition. I sent a second letter making the same request and asking if there was some good reason that the inspection report was not furnished me. I had the same response as in the first request.

I sent a third letter and a copy to Rep. Walt Mueller. I received a copy of the inspection report, not from the Highway Department, but from Rep. Mueller. The report was disturbing. Many components of the bridge were rated poor or very poor.

My position on the Municipal League's Executive Committee helped me gain a membership in the ad hoc East West Gateway Transportation Committee which made recommendations for highway improvements. With cooperation of others on that committee, the project for the new highway and new bridge was moved up to a more immediate time frame.

I wanted the Highway Department to re route the highway through the eastern part of Valley Park and of course have the new bridge farther east. The Highway Department would have none of it. The bridge would be replaced close to where it stood and many were unhappy about the choice and my support for it. I reasoned that if I made the inspection report public, it would cause people to avoid coming through the City and have an adverse impact on the businesses located along the route until the completion of a new bridge and new lanes entering and exiting. Of course, there was another argument that some businesses would have to be closed and bought out. It was a dilemma. My decision was to endorse the Highway Department proposal. Some said it cost me reelection. In retrospect, when I look at the intersection of Marshall and 141 rush hour traffic with three lanes in and out of the City and contemplate what it would be like with only one lane in and out of the City, I am satisfied that the choice was right.

During my tenure we had the first two successful annexations in the City's history and the right of way for the Frisco Railroad was taken over for maintenance by the City with a rental payment of one dollar per year. The City had some difficulty getting the Frisco to cut the grass along the property and the City turned it into something of a park.

Also noteworthy was my introduction of Harry Simpson to Wayne Kennedy, the County Parks/Recreation Director. Simpson County Park came into being. Under a federal program, Simpson donated half the property for the park and the County purchased the other half.

Chairing the Municipal League's Legislative Committee, we were able to get a simplified annexation law passed. It made it possible for a city to annex without an election where the owner(s) agreed to be annexed.

In 1979 the Board adopted a resolution commending C. C. Van Noy, President since 1979 of the Absorbent Cotton Company and more recently named The Beauty Care Company, for donating to the City a considerably sized tract of land to be used for the levy. That would make condemnation unnecessary for that parcel. The commendation was for generosity and cooperation with the City.

At its April 4 meeting in 1982, the Board approved unanimously a motion by Alderman Finder that the Lions Club be granted a one day beer license for a July 4 picnic. It was another example of the appreciation which the City

The History Of Valley Park

has had over the years for the work of the Lions Club in providing services to the community.

On April 21, 1982, the resignation of Virginia Hiscox became effective. Her resignation was accepted on a motion by Alderman Joe Finder with an amendment changing only the effective date of resignation. Virginia was the daughter of George Metal, the long time building inspector for the City and she was the wife of Raymond Hiscox, whose younger brother Harry, was a boyhood neighbor and friend of the author.

In 1963 Harold Rue sat in Ann's Café with some of the usual townsfolk who frequented the restaurant. He recalled that Tom Spencer (bricklaying contractor), and Lawrence Bolte (owner of Bolte's Market) were in the group. A cab driver came into the restaurant and announced that President Kennedy had been shot. "It was chilling," Harold said.

Throughout his working years, Harold was a general contractor and in his formative years he worked with his dad farming land rented from the Valley Park Land Company. He recalled the floods of 1945, 1951 and 1957. The 1945 flood came close to the time that Harold was on a street in his neighborhood and someone exited a house and yelled that "The war is over." When Harold wasn't working the farmland he was often shoveling coal in the family station.

He noted that "I was born in the same block I'm living in." He had a twin brother who died at the age of four months. There was another brother and four sisters.

Among his memories were the train rides to the school picnic at Forest Park Highlands, his service of 20 years on the Board of Aldermen and a similar number of years as a member of the Board of Directors of the Meramec Valley Bank.

When one serves the School Board as a member for eighteen years, eleven of which were as its President, it is genuine evidence of a desire to serve a community.

Added to that service was 20 years as Municipal Judge for the City of Valley Park. This is part of legacy of Charles Ford who received his degree in law from the University of Missouri in 1980. Earlier, in 1970 he began a three year service in the Marine Corps, where his dad, Lloyd (Junior) Ford had served in WWII. In 1995 he retired from the Naval Reserve as a Commandeer after service in the Navy's AG from 1981 to 1984.

His earliest recollection in life of Valley Park was his residence in Newtown where his family lived in a duplex with a long stairway to the second floor and he stared out in the evenings watching for his dad to arrive home.

The History Of Valley Park

Other memories are those of attending the Nazarene Church from where he remembered Mr. Curtis and Mr. Daines along with Jo Ann Tillison.

His family moved from the Newtown location to a residence along 141 and then to Inez Avenue, but never did he have a place other than Valley Park which he called home.

He recalled that his Uncle Coleman and Aunt Laverne purchased a barn look-a-like residence on Boyd Avenue. This was the former residence of "Granny Hicks" on the north side of Boyd Avenue at the foot of he hill going west just before the street climbs an equally long and equally steep hill going west.

In talking about boyhood friends, he mentioned John Riordan, Butch Wilkins, Kenny Barnett and Ricky Statler. In high school, he played in the band and on the basketball team and acquired a "good feeling" from the environment at VPHS. Mr. Gouty, although blind, was one who impressed him with dedication and a caring attitude toward his students.

At the turn of the Century he and his wife Karen (Moon) resided at a large home on the corner of Lookout and Fern Ridge.

Marlene (Harrington) Hedrick was mentioned earlier for her contributions to the history of Valley Park through the Meramec Station Historical Society and her untiring effort in the preservation of local history. She remembers, when four years old, her family lived on Front Street. That street parallels the old Frisco Railroad tracks just north of Marshall Avenue. She and her parents, Stan and Laura Harrington, lived in the first house north of the old Meramec Bank Building. Her grandparents, James and Emma O'Brien lived in the next house to the north and the third house was that of her uncle Bill O'Brien and wife.

She recalls that her grandpa was burning down an old shed and she was running to see Mr. Mueller and his horse. He delivered the Start-Times newspaper (it went out of business in 1951) and would let children feed carrots to his horse which pulled the buggy carrying the papers. She tripped and fell into the fire and burned herself enough that she had to make a trip to the hospital.

Her parents gave her assurance that one could do whatever the mindset determined, admonished her to be fair and treat everyone with respect, and urged her to remember that "You are no better than the next person. We all have to answer to the same maker."

The History Of Valley Park

Marlene has fond memories of Emma O'Brien, known to her many friends as "Sis," as a lady who helped anyone, worked for Meramec Valley Bank for 63 years, and walked to work every day. Emma was the first female to hold a City wide office, that of Treasurer. She was appointed to that office, serving after the passing of Harry Vance. Among others whom Marlene remembers – Mrs. Caroline Bibbs, a leader in the Afro-American community and Mrs. Ethyl Ralph, wife of Senator Richard Ralph. Ethyl was widowed and continued to serve the community in many ways, including service on the Valley Park Community Library Board of Trustees.

Marlene recalls the Mass at which Father Meyer announced that Japan had bombed Pearl Harbor. She also recalls the rationing of gas, sugar, coffee, shoes and other consumer goods.

Mr. Frank Swantner was the Civil Defense officer who, during WWII, at 8:00 p.m., would walk up and down the street to see if each of the homes had lights turned off. Marlene and her sister got under the covers and listened to Lux Theater, and other radio shows which sent popular brands of cigarettes to our servicemen overseas. Going to the Park Theatre, Grace's restaurant, and the old drug store are memories from the 50's.

Through The 20th Century

Marlene attended Eugene Coyle High School in Kirkwood (now St. Peters Elementary School). A number of casualties in the Korean War had been classmates of hers when she attended business college. She became a comptometer operator and later was employed by Southwestern Bell Telephone. She married Willard Hedrick and had two daughters and a son, the latter born in the 1960's. It was in that decade that she recalls Rock and Roll and Young's Ice Cream, followed by the Hippies into the 70's with the long hair, band "groups," a business, the loss of her dad, and the war in Viet Nam. An important mark in time for her was the beginning of the Meramec Station Historical Society, 1976. She and Alice Swantner, were movers in the Meramec Valley Historical Society and furnished timely articles in the City's newsletter with excerpts from Valley Park history.

In the 1980's her first grand daughter arrived and flooding in 1982 brought on losses to many and a move to the higher ground along Fern Ridge. Grand daughters number two and three arrived. More flooding came in the 1990's and the loss of her mother, her husband, and aunt. It was then that the initial invasion of Iraq took place. The 1990's saw arrival of Marlene's youngest granddaughter.

Donald Smith was born in Valley Park, one of a number of home grown products. His earliest recollections of Valley

The History Of Valley Park

Park include the Grover Johnson Blacksmith operation along St. Louis Avenue and the Komotos Shoe Store on Marshall, a short distance from the old Frisco Railroad tracks.

He remembers the flooding which took place at various times from 1945 to 1982 ('82 standing out in his memory), with the 1945 flood taking place when he "was a small boy." The people whom he remembers best are John Goree (Union Electric Company), Mr. Everett, Mr. James and Mr. Guy Tyrey. He cites as his fondest memories his days at Benton School and Valley Park High School. In High School his best friend was Nelson Corbin. "I had a car. Most kids did not." Lilly Botkins, history teacher, was his favorite teacher. That train ride to Forest Park Highlands for the school picnic is among his fondest memories. He notes that his dad was gone "for four years" during World War II in the U. S. Navy. He was in the military himself starting in 1952 in the Army and was sent to Korea.

He and his wife, Patricia (Cary) Smith, became parents of two sons, Andrew and Jeffrey. He was employed by the City in the Water Department in 1982, worked there for 35 years and returned on a part time basis two years after retiring. He recalls Lake Hill, Arnold's Grove, the Valley Park Hotel and the old Mission. The latter was an old Indian Mission with a concrete-stucco exterior adjacent Highway

141 toward the river and close to it between the river and Arnold's Drive.

Gary Adams remembered early days of the Lions Club meetings when Bill Menner (he became owner of Weggeman's Grocery at the corner of Marshall and 141) used to bring food and drinks to the meeting and after the meeting, the members all helped in devouring it. He noted that the meetings and the sessions after the meetings, were both enjoyable.

Only business people were supposed to be members and Adams was uncertain why he, not being a business man, was permitted to join. "I was still on active duty in the Army when I became a member of the Lions. My brother Kenny Adams, introduced me to the Lions and encouraged me to join.

The Lions were always pro-active in the community. Many young people who could not afford eyeglasses, had them provided by the Lions and there were many other forms of help given to those in need, including payments for surgery in some cases. Adams also recalled the Christmas parties and the Easter egg hunts provided for the town's children. There were also the talent shows where participants would sing or do a dance or some other performance.

The History Of Valley Park

The Weggeman boys, Bernie and Clarence, took part in the construction of the Lions building by helping with the transport of logs from the Ranken estate along the old Highway 66 just west of where 141 intersects it. Adams indicated that the Weggeman brothers hauled the logs to the Meramec, and then floated them downstream where they were retrieved and hauled the remaining distance from the Meramec to the Pyramid and Kena Street area adjacent the building site and then to their destination. Adams always thought that Valley Park was one of the greatest places to live in his formative years and he returned to Valley Park after 21 years in the Army. During that time he noted changes in the old business district and observed, "But the people hadn't changed. If you needed something, people in Valley Park would deliver. I raised both my kids here. Both of them graduated from Valley Park High, both honor students, and we were fortunate to have William Gouty as one of the finest teachers ever." Adams and his wife, Dana, remembered Gouty as one of the finest people you could know. "Even though he was blind, Gouty loved to go to the ball games and my son took him a number of times."

Gary Adams's dad moved to Valley Park in 1906 from St. James, Missouri.

"I remember that the Christmas parties and the Easter egg hunts put on by the Lions were major attractions. The

Through The 20th Century

Lions often gave baskets of food and candies to kids at Christmas and for many, it was the only Christmas the kids had. People always looked up to the Lions in this town because the Lions served. Well, we do serve."

These were among the thoughts of Joe Schulte, a long time Lions member and activist in the community, joining in 1968. He expressed regret that it was difficult to get younger folks to get involved as members of the Lions.

The BBQ's and other activities were promoted by young folks over the past but there doesn't seem to be as much interest on the part of the young to get involved now. "One of the things that can't be taken away as a recognition of good, is the people in our Lions organization. Hopefully we will attract more of the young to keep things going." Joe echoed sentiments of others who believed that Valley Park. was a good place to grow up"… as a youngster I remember playing ball in the field behind our house. That was where everyone played."

Mary Young (her friends call her Toot or Tootie) was born in Valley Park, August 28, 1941, in her family home.

Her father was Charles Lee Lindsey whose birthplace was Cruise, Missouri, and he was born on December 26,1912. His wife Mildred (Bradley) Lindsey was born in Swiften, Arkansas, January 2, 1920. Mary's twin sisters

The History Of Valley Park

were Charlene and Edwina. An older brother was Norman and two younger brothers were Robert and Joseph…

"My earliest recollection of Valley Park as a young child was playing around my house – we were not allowed to leave the block we lived on. One of my favorite things was playing paper dolls with the girl next door, she had store bought paper dolls and mine were cut out of the Sears catalog. We also played games in the yard, like "red light, green light," and "mother may I" and other games. My brother Norman had a large can of marbles. Sometimes he let me play with those marbles.

The people she most remembers were neighbors – . The Crane family, McGraw family, the Stewarts, Bransons, Kellys and her paternal grandparents. Her Aunt Ollie Lindsey Thomas was another. Ann and Frank Cuchetti ran the corner market and "were so good to our family."

Mary's mother and her neighbors talked about different young men who served in the Korean conflict. Her husband Paul was born on May 22, 1940. He recalls a fire in the Woodenwar factory sometime in the mid or late '50's and another fire in 1961 at the American Brokerage (formerly Wolf's Department Store on Meramec Station Road just north of Dan Wolfe's garage). He remembers Komotos shoe repair store on Marshall and the Kroger Store (later an IGA store owned by Lawrence Bolte). Mary and Paul were married about the time of the outbreak of the Viet Nam War. Paul was in the Air Force and they lived in Minot, North Dakota. He served in the Air Force for four years and worked as an electrician in his civilian life. As of the year 2000 he had served in that occupation for forty two years. Paul never had to go to the war zone. Mary noted that TV pictures of those "being killed on both sides" were terrible and there were more "terrible" pictures appearing when the U. S. pulled out.

School days at Benton School hold fond memories. "We walked to school and most days walked home for lunch, On special days we got to take a sack lunch and buy a bottle of milk." Playground was the best thing, like great swings, playing dodge ball with Brenda Halsey, Judy Blankenship, Barbara Stewart and many other friends. Entering middle school, we still had to walk almost every day regardless of the weather. In middle school the circle of friends enlarged and Sandy Boyd became a great friend.

In high school years a favorite thing was hanging out in the Coffee Pot, on the northeast corner of Vance and old Hywy 141. Mary, Judy Blankenship, Brenda Halsey, Dorothy Reeves, Sandy Boyd, Iva James, and others played the juke box and danced. Swimming at White Mineral Swimming Pool and watching races at Lakehill Speedway were other favorites along with an occasional shopping trip on the bus to Kirkwood or Maplewood.

Mary loved her cheerleading role and watching the basketball games...

She remembers what she called a great trip with Class of '59 graduates to the east coast and Canada. In her freshman year she had started working in the cafeteria and had her lunch free. The workers there "were so nice to me, but they were nice to everyone." A real treat arrived when the Coca Cola man would come to school and everyone got a free coke. Favorite meals in the cafeteria were the peanut butter sandwiches and the chili, served on special days.

An event near the end of the forties is remembered when a train wreck spilled a load of Hershey bars. "I think every kid in my neighborhood had Hershey candy for a while." Mary referred to the levee project as a significant development. "I know having your home full of water is heartbreaking." The schools "have improved and I have three grandchildren attending them." Throughout Valley Park's history a most important thing has to be "...its people." Living in a small town you "...know the people, sometimes good and sometimes bad, but they would always help another person."

Through The 20th Century

I hope the young people of Valley Park keep coming back. They are the future of our town. Four of my five grandchildren have made their homes here which pleases me very much... love having the grandkids so close." About current pursuits... gardening... love working in my yard, playing cards with friends, and spending time with family. I am still learning on the computer with some days "better than others."

Jack Dietz indicated his earliest memory of Valley Park was moving from St. Louis at the age of six. He remembered seeing a large sphinx on Pharoah Drive and an office inside of it for real estate operations. "We had lived in the City of St. Louis and came out to Valley Park periodically. My uncle owned 30 acres which is now Simpson Lake. We moved here permanently since we had three houses out here. We moved here with our little girl Kathy in 1951."

"In 1955, Lou Brown and I built our houses on Meramec Station Road."

"I served as a police officer and later as clerk of the Police Court. Lot of changes – new highway and removal of the old stores... Carol House bought the old Lumber yard and Cuchetti's market. I have been here 58 years ... a good place to live... once in a while we had some rough times but all in all...." Marge Dietz remembers the small

The History Of Valley Park

town, or country town flavor. "I always remember the people of Valley Park, the greatest people in the world." Then Jack continued, "Late 50's or early 60's we had a lion in Valley Park," he said. "I was a police officer at the time and answered the call about a lion and drove out Vance and sounded the siren at a low pitch. It was loud enough to disturb the lion which stampeded Sprock's cattle. They ran out on Vance Road and Lou Brown (then Chief of Police) told me immediately after, 'You ever do something like that again, I'll kill you.'" It was not a genuine threat but served to illustrate the displeasure on the part of Chief Brown who also said, "You get that lion out of town, I don't care how. I don't know how you are going to do it, but you get rid of it." "I called the zoo and asked to speak to an official there. Someone answered the phone and I told him about the lion and that I needed a suggestion. He told me, 'I don't want to hear about your lion' and hung up on me. Then a couple of guys knew someplace in Illinois where the lion would be welcomed so the City was relieved of the lion problem. I don't know where he ended up in Illinois but was glad to be rid of him."

Jack gave a chuckle about a joke directed at him when the guys used to gather in a local restaurant for some small talk. One of the members of the group called it the "Liar's Club." That was Bob Vance. Jack was a foreman for Rossi

Plumbing in St. Louis and told of his crew digging up old cast iron sewer pipes to install new ones. A rat's nest was uncovered and the rats ran in all directions. One of them ran into a section of cast iron pipe and got stuck. A worker pulled him out, hit him over the head and killed him. The worker put the rat on a scale and told Jack, "That thing weighed eighteen pounds." After two or three others of those present contributed stories, Bob Vance noted fishing upstream in a big hole on the Meramec with Bob Seville. The two were recognized as among the best or maybe the best fishermen in town. They saw this big head come to the edge of the water near sundown and decided to bait for him. They put out a line from a limb overhanging the water and baited it. About 2:30 in the morning the branch was thrashing the water. They rowed out and Bob said, "When I pulled him up and his head broke water, he flipped over, broke our line and knocked my flashlight out of my hand. We lost the fish and my flashlight. We baited for him again the next night and about 3:00 in the morning the branch was thrashing the water again. This time I took my grab hook with me and put it against the side of the fish, ran it up into his gills and pulled him in. We had him. We strung him up, cut him open and he had swallowed my flashlight which was still burning." Jack Dietz said, "Bob, you must have imagined that. Batteries won't operate in the high acid

The History Of Valley Park

of a fish's stomach." Bob said, "Well, Jack, if you take ten pounds off your rat, I'll turn off my flashlight."

John Brust,was a member of the Lions for about twenty five years, enjoyed most the experience of helping people. He remembers eyeglasses in particular, but hearing aids, diabetic treatment and many other ways of giving assistance to those in need. His wife Joyce, is a Lady Lion, and as noted the Lady Lions have become a major ingredient in the service of the Lions to the community.

Brust served on the City Council and expresses concern about people making improvements to their property in the City. "It's hard for improvements to be made quickly when people can't afford it. We can't pressure people too much to (structurally) improve. It's satisfying to try to 'hold up' for the needs of people while in government. Once you get into politics, it's kind of hard to get out of it."

Joe Harrington was born in 1942 and remembers when James O'Brien, former Marshal, lived with his family. His uncle, Art O'Brien, was the proprietor of O'Brien's Buffet on Marshall Road and he recalls another Marshal, Gus Cox. A fond memory of his includes the Lake Hill Speedway and the auto races there. While in high school, he worked for John Kovac.

Through The 20th Century

Joe graduated from CBC High School in 1960 and entered the U. S. Navy under the "buddy system" which kept two enlistees together for most of the time served in the Navy. His "buddy system" participant was John Kovac, Jr. After six years service in the Navy, he married the former Judy Ford and they had an addition to their family in 1970 and another in 1974. Their residence was on Quinwood.

In 1976 he was elected to the Valley Park School Board and served until 1996 including the latter 10 years as President of the Board. During his tenure on the School Board, planning took place for an extensive building or remodeling program. The older middle school was replaced and a new industrial arts shop and band building was constructed. In preparation for the industrial arts/band building, springs were discovered in the water table and piling had to be sunk well below ground level to establish a sound foundation. We have to wonder if this area might have been one of the sulfur springs mentioned in the City's early history. Harrington remembered that a "spring" also was found on the Sacred Heart Church grounds. The two locales were across old Highway 141 from each other. At the Sacred Heart School, Joe remembered Sister Imelda as a favorite among his teachers.

He was elected Mayor in 1994, a year in which a flash flood occurred and he was sworn in as Mayor in the Methodist

The History Of Valley Park

Church because of damage to the City Hall Building. Valley Days, in '95 and '96 were held on the land bordering the Big Bend-Dougherty Ferry intersection. He noted that the Meramec River has had an important place in the life of the City. Thinking about the potential completion of a levy, he hoped to see an extensive industrial and/or commercial development somewhere within the flood protected land.

A ringing testimonial favoring Valley Park is provided by Ed Sidwell.

He is a former police officer in Valley Park and made an interesting observation about the City when he recalled a Post-Dispatch article that said if a tornado came through Kansas and lifted a small town, then deposited it in west St. Louis County, the transplant would describe Valley Park.

When he first moved to Valley Park he could not help being impressed by the generosity of the people. Neighbors helped carry in belongings when he "moved in." That, and the courtesies he found, made him decide that he "wouldn't want to leave this community." Ed became involved in real estate and construction and acquired a considerable amount of property in Valley Park. In the nineties, he served on the Board of Aldermen.

MORE CITY BUSINESS

Alderman Harold Rue moved and Alderman David Cusack seconded a motion to approve a tailgate sale by the Lady Lions with a waiver of fee. That was April 1, 1983. The Lady Lions had joined with their male counterparts in providing services to the community and the tailgate sale was one of the means by which funds were raised to carry out those services.

Alderman Joe Finder moved in December of 1983, to give Jean (Shepherd) Grellner the gavel which Judge Richard Grellner had used during his term as City Police Court Judge. That motion had a second from Alderman Rue and carried unanimously.

March 20, 1985, the Board met in a special meeting to discuss planning for possible emergency in case of flooding. Aldermen Adams, Beckett, and Chief Brown were appointed to work with the Corps of Engineers and make additional plans for actions, including evacuation, to be taken in the event of disastrous flooding.

The City had for some time had an interest in the land area to the northeast of the City limits and on June 6, 1985,

The History Of Valley Park

a resolution was adopted to indicate intent to annex the area generally described as the land area adjacent the Dougherty Ferry-Big Bend intersection.

A letter to the Board on August 3, 1987, was received complaining about vandalism on the railroad viaduct. Pam Kettler introduced a motion to have the City post a $100 reward for arrest and conviction of anyone putting graffiti on the railroad viaducts. The motion was seconded and carried unanimously.

On the heels of information regarding a possible annexation by or merger with the Parkway and/or Rockwood School Districts, Alderwoman Pam Kettler asked that it be recorded that she had no interest in and was not a part of the effort to petition for Valley Park Schools to become part of Rockwood or Parkway. Her request was on August 19, 1987.

The Board of Aldermen in November of 1987 took opposition by resolution to County Executive Gene McNary's plan for consolidation of St. Louis County municipalities.

June 2, 1997, the City denied a proposal for the City employees to wear shorts during the work-a-day activities. Employees had requested this but the denial carried unanimously. That request came from Cindy Stamper, an assistant City Clerk to whom the employees appealed. Unable to make that kind of decision, she brought it to the Board along with a list of bids in case the City wished to accept the plan.

An ordinance was passed in the 90's regulating towers and antennas showing that the City was recognizing the high tech age. And it was during the nineties that City employees were sent to workshops on use of computer technology.

July 14, 1997, the Board received a letter from Mr. Ed Sidwell who had been employed by the City earlier as a police officer. His letter suggested that a 10 cents per hour increase should not be passed, pointing out that this amounted to only four dollars per week. Sidwell suggested also that the City might have just frozen wages which would have shown more respect for employees rather than a decision to give such a small increase.

It was sometimes necessary for the City to seek the County's cooperation in the matter of planning for the levy. On July 17, 1990, St. Louis County passed an ordinance, moved by Councilman Quinn to instruct the County Executive to grant a 60 ft. easement for a 48" storm sewer to pass through Simpson Park.

July 21, 1997, the Board voted to transfer $7,500 from the sales tax fund as a loan to the TIF fund TIF or Tax

The History Of Valley Park

Increment Financing fund. The latter was a plan whereby a defined area could have developments free from realty taxes for a prescribed period. This provided an inducement for a developer to make improvements and have those improvements free from real estate taxes for a period indicated. That measure was debated and passed by a vote of 5-2.

August 4, 1997, there was discussion about the possible hiring of a City Administrator. It seems to have been an idea whose time hadn't come and there was no action taken in that direction. It was moved and seconded that same August 4, 1997, that streets in Glen Eagles, Mission Hills and Dougherty Ferry Woods be accepted by the City for maintenance. The attorney was to draw an ordinance for presentation at the next meeting. The streets became the obligation of the City for maintenance.

Observations of Laura J. Kinder, who became Superintendent of Valley Park Schools after the turn of the Century, gives insight to a newcomer's perception. "The first time I came to Valley Park was to interview for a position as assistant principal in the Valley Park School District. Having moved to St. Louis County ten months earlier the flood of 1994 had already come and gone only a few weeks before I visited the school campus, and I remember thinking how remarkable it was that the buildings showed no signs of the waters. I was also impressed with the students, staff, and parents who participated in the interviews. Everyone was so positive and friendly. Being in Valley Park felt like being in a small town in Missouri, something I had ample experience with since I had lived most of my life in the bootheel of our state."

"During the twelve years I have had the privilege to work in the Valley Park School District, the school district has undergone considerable change. Valley Park Elementary School and Dennis R. Lea Early Childhood Center were constructed and Valley Park Middle School and High School were remodeled. The use of technology as a learning tool is integrated throughout our program, and our students have a greater degree of access to technology than in most school districts in our state. Our beautiful campus is a source of pride for the community, and we often hear praise from others outside our district on our facilities as well as our academic program. Our citizens have provided an outstanding level of support in order to make this possible." Laura Kinder became the first female to serve as Valley Park Superintendent of Schools.

Dan Adams, born in 1961, recalled in his early days how a new City truck, driven by City employee Tom Downey, was thought to be owned by Mr. Downey who did nothing

The History Of Valley Park

to discourage the belief and may have inadvertently even encouraged it.

Dan's family moved here from Kentucky when the Chrysler Plant came to the St. Louis area in 1959 and the family lived on Leonard Street over the years. His father served in the military in WWII prior to Dan's birth and would not say much about his wartime experiences until the last two years of his life. Dan recalled the many floods and the practice of having boat races on "our own private lake." (That would be the "lake" formed over Leonard Street.)

He recalled the assassination of Martin Luther King and the landing on the moon in the sixties. He referred to the 70's as the long hair era and "If you see my high school picture you would know I was part of it."

Mayor Adams presided over the transfer of police protection in 1999 to St. Louis County and noted, "The challenges for our police were too much. We could not handle control of the drug trafficking and the accompanying costs."

He had made his entry into the political arena by speaking at a hearing in Sacred Heart Church. It was about a proposal for a TIF and he recalls filing for office when Glenn Moon was the City Clerk. Mayor Adams served from 1998 to 2000 and recalled how Mr. William Gouty, history teacher, engaged in conferences with him. "The first time donation to my campaign came from Eileen Sherril," another history teacher He would choose not to run again because of the terminal illness on the part of both parents. His best memories included receiving news of the funding for our levy and the moves toward its completion.

The History Of Valley Park

PERSONAL NOTE

In our home, an evening reading from the Bible was a ritual and each of us took our own turns at reading.

This was especially beneficial to me in that when I enrolled in school, I was already reading with far more proficiency than would have otherwise been the case. The King James version of the Bible is not easy reading and it gave me the ability to handle the written word without great effort. All 12 years of my elementary and secondary schooling were in the Valley Park Schools.

In 1951, I graduated from Northeast Missouri State (later named Truman State U.), married Doris Ruth DeClue in August and was inducted into the Army on October 19. I arrived at Camp Roberts, California, after a stop at Camp Crowder, Missouri

Every person who has served in the military knows most of the story. "Cover down, cover down," yelled Sergeant Pappas. "The goats on my uncle's farm can form a line better than you guys. Now! When I blow this whistle, I want you to come out of that barracks door two abreast. If you can't make it, leave a little blood and hair on the door frame so I know you tried." And so it went.

Near the end of basic training I tried out for and made the regimental basketball team which would compete for the post championship. I felt like I "peaked" in my playing very close to the end of my senior year of college. We won the post championship and would next play for the southern division of the Sixth Army Area championship and we won that.

A tougher test came in determining the championship of the Sixth Army Area. There was anxiety for me in that Doris was pregnant with our son, Dale, and I hadn't heard for a time as to how she was doing. At half time, Ft. Lewis, Washington, winner of the northern Sixth Army Area championship, was ahead of us. I had 9 points during the first half. At half time, Lt. Hurley came into the dressing room and indicated that the Red Cross had made contact with my home folks and found that Doris was doing fine. What a relief! In the second half I scored 18 points and we won going away. I felt good about the game because "my man" on the Ft. Lewis team was John Wilson who had played for the Harlem Globetrotters.

Through some maneuvering, we picked up Scottie Steagall, a little All American out of Milliken U. and Frank

The History Of Valley Park

Kuzara, All American out of the U. of San Francisco We went to San Antonio, Texas, to play in the World Wide All Army Tourney at Briggs Army Medical Base, Ft. Sam Houston, Texas. In the double elimination tourney, we won the championship as the only undefeated entry. General Partridge sent us orders to go on Temporary Duty (TDY) for 2 weeks but did not specify in the order where to report except to report to our home base of Camp Roberts at the end of 2 weeks. So, in the absence of a directive as to where to spend the 2 weeks of TDY, we went home. At Camp Roberts, General Partridge addressed us outside his Commanding Officer's quarters and congratulated us on our win.

I was later sent to the Armed Forces Information School at Ft. Slocum, N. Y., and then returned to Camp Roberts where I played baseball, held troop information conferences, prepared news releases, edited a regimental newspaper, and took magazines, news round-ups to read and recordings to play to troops on bivouac – my only experience as a kind of disc jockey and newscaster. We were fortunate to have a newswire service in our headquarters unit with hourly or sometimes more frequent printouts of news roundups. The Army turned me loose in October, 1953, and two weeks after my discharge, I was teaching at Pacific, Missouri, High School where a vacancy had occurred.

Through The 20th Century

I taught at Pacific High and the following year began teaching in Valley Park and finished my secondary school teaching at Kirkwood High. I was in Kirkwood for 26 years. After teaching nine years at the University of Missouri-St. Louis, I left to give full time care to my wife, Doris, who had pancreatic cancer and we would lose the battle with cancer on Christmas Eve, 2001.

During my teaching, I served as a delegate many times to the National Education Association Representatrive Assembly and was a charter member of the Missouri NEA. I was part of a seven member commission invited by the Washington State Education Association to study and report on educational finance in that state. It involved a one week visit and a follow up weekend visit leading to preparation of a report and recommendations. Another great opportunity came in the form of serving on the NEA Government Relations Committee which involved many trips to Washington, D. C., and visits to Congressional Offices over a four year period.

At this writing, a son and a daughter, Dale and Karen, are married and live in the St. Louis area and there are seven grandchildren.

The History Of Valley Park

POST SCRIPT

In the year 2000, kids had long since stopped swimming in Fish Pot Creek, Grand Glaize Creek or the Meramec River. There are more sedentary pastimes messing with electronic games of one kind or another.

The old Lake Hill Speedway which replaced one of the earlier lakes and furnished a training ground for Kenny Wallace, the race car driver, is gone. No longer were trains stopping daily to pick up passengers to take them to work or delivering passengers at the end of a work day.

The old Mo Pac station is no more and the only remnant is the pillars on which the station sat just northeast of Highway 141, on the opposite side of the track from Forest Avenue. The Frisco depot is likewise gone.

The Meramec River flows merrily on with the promise, in 2000, of a soon-to-be completed levee to control the waters when the river would otherwise become hostile.

The High School basketball team long since left the confines of the little cracker box gym and the entry to the high school and school administration has changed from an address at 356 Meramec Station Road to one at 111 Main Street. Many of the people whose names appear in this account, are still around

Students no longer dance in the Study Hall during lunch period as they got permission to do, as Dolores (Uhles) McKinney, Class of '47, recalled. David Lochman looked back at the school year 59-60 when the school bus broke down carrying the basketball team to Steelville, Missouri, and Carl Vires was called to pick up all the passengers he could, a total of five. The team had to play the entire game with only five players.

In 1967, the Ft. Zumwalt Basketball Tournament was won by Valley Park and stands out in the memory of Danny Cook. Patty "Poppe" Polster was one of a number of students who went door to door to register opposition to the proposal for Valley Park Schools to become part of the Rockwood School District. Some students went on a strike, Danny Fowler among them. Then Superintendent John Cleary noted that he had been advised of the intent of the students and did not object. "They were simply frustrated," he said.

The admonition that cigarettes were "coffin nails" from Henry Williams, the longtime teacher in Valley Park Schools, gained significant acceptance as the Twentieth Century came to a close with increasing importance assigned to a a smoke free environment.

The Wilson Stove Factory which sat near the railroad siding just east of the old Frisco mainline, is gone and a remnant – an old Wilson Stove, sat in the main corridor of the City Hall at the turn of the Century. It was received by Marlene (Harrington) Hedrick on behalf of the Meramec Valley Historical Society.

Tom and Donna Rauls were long time movers in the Parent Teacher Organization. They purchased a resort in the Branson area and operated it for some time before selling it and returning to Valley Park.

Don and Cynthia (Cindy) Taylor were long time residents of Valley Park and then moved to California where Don had a new job. They owned property at the intersection of Quinwood and Jefferson and the property was three lots deep on the south side of Quinwood. After Cindy became widowed, she donated the two deeper lots to the Valley Park School District and the Don and Cynthia Wildlife Preserve named in their honor is maintained by Valley Park Schools.

Many of the alumni from VPHS at the turn of the Century still prefer Young's as the site for their reunions and several have had reunions there. Young's has returned

Through The 20th Century

to near its older location west of 141 near the old Missouri Pacific R.R. after a stay along old Highway 141 until the new Highway 141 right-of-way claimed it.

A noticeable unchanged feature of the City is that people are still aware of problems of others, translate that awareness into caring, and translate the caring into a helping hand.

In putting this account together, notices were placed on the VPHS High School Alumni web site with solicitations for memories of Valley Park, and some responded, but not as many as hoped for.

Mailing of a questionnaire to a considerable number of residents brought some responses and hand delivered questionnaires brought a good number of responses, but again, not as many as hoped for. Too many people believe they cannot contribute to a work of this kind, not realizing how there is something within each individual's history which contributes to an overall account.

Hopefully, another account of Valley Park History beyond the 20th Century will bring an even more in depth view of life in Valley Park in the new Century and additions to accounts of the 20th.